AF255743

COPYRIGHT

Copyright © 2022 by Dr. Darlington Akaiso

All rights reserved. Without the written permission of the publisher, no part of this book may be reproduced or used in any way (graphic, electronic and mechanical, including photocopying, recording) except for the use of brief quotes by book reviewers.

Publication data on file with National Library and Archives Canada

ISBN: 978-0-578-34933-6

Published by Soyounique Press
www.soyounique.ca

DISCLAIMER

All the work and opinions expressed herein are those of the author alone. They do not represent the opinion of any of the establishments with which the author is associated. Hence, no other party should be attributed to any errors of the fact of any kind related to this publication.

ABOUT THE AUTHOR

Dr. Darlington Akaiso is an academic scholar. He has written numerous books on global security and leadership studies. For over twenty years, he has worked in risk management, resilience planning, and international development. He has also taught in various capacities at the Northeastern University, University of Manitoba, Seneca College, Trent University in Canada, and the University of the West Indies in the Caribbean. He earned his bachelor's degree in Information Technology/Informatics from York University, Toronto, Canada, his master's degree in Management Information Systems from the University of Illinois-Springfield, USA, and his doctorate in Leadership from Franklin Pierce University, New Hampshire, USA. He is also an alumnus of the Massachusetts Institute of Technology (MIT), USA, and Harvard Kennedy School, Cambridge, MA, USA.

AUTHOR'S NOTE

Nigeria is one of the most linguistically diverse nations in the world, and while English is the official language, harkening back to colonial days, it is not the most common and rarely the only one spoken.

The country has been resource-rich and at the center of international trade for centuries, and as a result, you can hear over 500 languages regularly in use today. Nigerians are collectively multilingual, and many can switch, for example, from Hausa to Igbo to English on a dime.

The quotes you will read in this book often come directly from Nigerian media, and much of the syntax will not be the formal American English you see in the rest of the book. The quotes are left as published, without grammatical adjustment or a confusing plethora of "*[sic]*". This is done with both the writers and readers in mind, in hopes that a cross-cultural understanding of linguistic norms can be respectfully established within.

ABOUT THE BOOK

While reminiscing over Professor Thomas N. Kibua's masterpiece, *A History of Kenya's Endemic Corruption Virus*, I was left with no choice but to conclude that the Corruption Virus has really infested the entire African continent. Indeed, it was through his work that I was inspired to write about such a difficult subject.

Out of ten Nigerian politicians, eleven are corrupt?

A convicted money launderer welcomed home with a parade. Another, a governor, widely celebrated for escaping Europe in a dress and on a forged passport. Seventy million naira allegedly swallowed by snakes and monkeys.

In this book, I meticulously outline the appalling extent to which the powerful few work behind the scenes to shamelessly plunder the resources of Nigeria. Up to eight billion dollars is lost annually to corruption, and no politician goes unexamined in this piercing review.

From jungle justice to the corrupt kleptocracy that defines Nigeria's ruling class today, I clearly give historical context to a modern but untenable problem. This important record speaks truth to power and documents the crushing consequences of political gaming. It is a must-read for any student of justice, ethics, and politics in the world.

TABLE OF CONTENT

CHAPTER ONE

Introduction: From Democracy To Kleptocracy

There is an underground language in Nigeria, and it is coded inextricably into the systems of politics and governance. It is neither written nor openly spoken; instead it remains in its unique and shrouded state. Those who are fluent are loath to follow rules. In Nigeria, this is the language of corruption.

This lingua franca is ever present but mainly comes alive in official circumstances. Those who have good command of it use it widely to subvert the rules of honest and transparent leadership and instead squeeze the most out of the people's system. The adept may be perceived as cerebral and experienced, both in statecraft and in politics, and as a result there is much they get away with. The language of corruption can imbue its shrewd master with the blind admiration of those who don't have the golden tongue. A corrupt politician, in its use, can gain swift advantage. He is a force to be reckoned with in his parliamentary schemes.

Others - those who speak of meritocracy, transparency, and due process - are scoffed at and viewed as unsuitable; the incorruptible hardly last, construed as misfits and kept at bay by mainstream politicians who speak that other language. No one wants spoilers around, and everyone wants to be safe. Hence, more often than not, the ones considered incorruptible are set up and eased out of the system. Any political office holder who wants to be safe or be relevant has to understand the unspoken language governing the game of politics, the language that conveys the craftiness, shrewdness, and mastery expected of an experienced politician.

In understanding the nexus between politics and corruption, we must first understand the definition of the former as summed up in the title of Harold Lasswell's 1936 book Politics: Who Gets What, When, and How. According to Muhammad Zahid, this definition "has encapsulated political behavior around the world, with politicians being driven by political positions, resource distribution and out-competing their competitors."[1]

Put differently, the set of activities involved in making collective decisions - and in fostering relationships in terms of distribution of power and resources - involves making moves both inside and outside the law.. And because of politicians' seemingly inherent compulsion to outshine their peers, some too easily stoop to breaking lawful limits in order to gain advantage. This misplaced and overzealous competition, gone unchecked, has become modus operandi for the typical Nigerian politician. The end result is corruption.

According to Ilufoye Ogundiya of Usmanu Danfodiyo University, corruption is inextricably tied (but not limited) to politics, especially if politics is defined from the Lasswell's "who gets what, when and how" and perhaps how much.[2] Ogundiya adds that the struggle over resources otherwise known as the "national cake" in the Nigerian society has taken a debilitating toll.[3] He further paints the picture that "the idea that the 'national cake' is meant to be shared rather than baked, by the various ethnic groups that constitute Nigerian federation provides a fertile ground for the kleptomaniac individuals who are obsessed to siphoning the public fund."[4]

Why is corruption a political language? Because politics is a spectrum that must be ruled by its own language. Like the fields of law, medicine, and entertainment, politics is governed by a unique set of ethics, jargon, and idiosyncrasy. And because it revolves around competition for power, politicians seek to dominate rivals by flouting established rules and cutting corners for their own advantage. They operate with the cryptic language of deceit, false pretense, blackmail, intimidation, and falsification. They loot public funds and consider anything that contradicts the law.

These are means to an end: politicians understand that the

acquisition, expansion, and retention of power trump morality, and therefore they see nothing wrong with employing illegitimate means. In Nigeria, the words of politicians are often equated with lies and empty promises; they are deceptive speeches that serve as the syntax of the language of corruption.

Politicians understand when to bribe to get vital documents or to get appropriate authorities to look the other way; they understand that they need to accumulate vast wealth to show power; they understand the need to say and do whatever will gain them the popularity needed to triumph in the next election. Since none of these are guaranteed under legitimate circumstances, political elites indulge in the violation of established rules, making private gains through illegal means at the expense of the general public.

Corruption has perpetuated in Nigeria's system in a way that it has become both a norm and a culture. The most vexing aspect is that it keeps rising steadily and expanding with successive administrations. There was a time Nigerians thought democracy would offer improvement in their circumstances, but that has not yet come to pass. One example is how democracy played out after Sani Abacha's military regime from 1993 to 1998, which is often considered to be the apogee of corruption and where an estimated $4 billion to $5 billion was reported to have been looted and siphoned abroad. The economy was in shambles. The country suffered a dearth of infrastructure, and poverty became commonplace. According to Peter Lewis, "the depredations of the Abacha regime were extraordinary. Erratic policies, mismanagement and unabashed pillage by senior officials fomented slow growth and declining standards of living. The economic malaise dissipated the middle class, intensified communal tensions and weakened an already feeble state apparatus."[5]

At that time, the popular demand for democracy was fueled by hopes that accountability, transparency, and other niceties of civilian rule would put an end to financial incivility and restore economic development ruined by long periods of military junta. Abacha's death in 1998 paved the way for a return to democracy in 1999. Nigerians have lived under the guise of it but nominally ever since.

Democracy is supposed to be a form of government in which the people elect their leaders and hold them accountable. The Nation commentator Tochukwu Ezukanma contends that a dividend of democracy is power. All elected and appointed officials and every institution of government should act in accordance with their people's will, he says, noting that the powers of the governing be subordinated to the will of the governed.[6] Those entrusted with power in a democracy are expected to be transparent.

It is thus paradoxical that a democratic system that promotes accountability and transparency has become a hotbed for corruption. Since 1999, corruption has become endemic in Nigeria's public system and its democracy has degenerated to kleptocracy. In the kleptocratic system, officials use the power they acquire by democratic means to misappropriate and embezzle public funds at the expense of the larger population. Like typical kleptomaniacs who live with an uncontrollable drive to steal, Nigerian politicians are constantly bent on looting public funds. The democratic system in the country has been perverted by systematic theft. According to Adisa, "it becomes an indisputable facts that Nigerian government under majority of our rulers (calling themselves leaders) are ruling us with kleptocracy in disguise of democracy, because it crystal clear that they have in no time to exhibit major tenets/ features of democracy except regular and periodic elections which supposed to be free, fair and credible but which has always been do or die by using power of incumbency to retain and perpetuate themselves or imposed their preferred candidates in power against the interest of the electorates."[7]

A kleptocracy occurs when corruption becomes an integrated and essential aspect of the economic, social, and political system such that honesty becomes irrational. It forces participants to follow what otherwise would be termed unacceptable ways, and actually punishes those who resist.[8]   In other words, violators are protected, and when exposed, treated leniently; their accusers are intimidated and victimized for exposing organizational hypocrisy.[9]

Those in positions of power have rendered the country a black hole of corruption. Even before the state formation of what is now called Nigeria, the people of this geo-political area faced the devastating consequences of it. Thus, at the time of independence, corruption was nothing new for Nigerians, and it has continued over the years to increase.

The United Nations Office on Drugs and Crime points out that "by some estimates, close to US $400 billion was stolen between 1960 and 1999."[10] From 1999 through 2007 when Olusegun Obasanjo was in power, Nigeria's government earned an estimated $223 billion due to rising oil revenue in the international market. The country, however, lost a minimum of $4 billion to $8 billion annually to corruption,[11] a figure that equates to between 4.25 percent and 9.5 percent of Nigeria's total GDP in 2006.[12]

From 1999 to the time of this writing, the estimated total of looted funds looks very sketchy. Emerging lists of recovered funds in 2018 might serve as an index to the extent of plundering by political elites. Along with Abacha's records of recovered bounty, the two lists published by Minister of Information Lai Mohammed on March 30, 2018 and April 1, 2018 were highly controversial. The main opposition party, the Peoples' Democratic Party (PDP), accused the All Progressives Congress (APC), who led the federal government at the time, of political witch-hunting. They described the lists as "a cheap blackmail as none of those listed had been indicted or convicted by any court of competent jurisdiction or any panel of enquiry in our country."[13] Below is the list of the alleged looters released on March 30, 2018:

- Uche Secondus, PDP chairman: on the February 19, 2015, he took N200 million from the office of the National Security Adviser (NSA)
- Former PDP financial secretary: on October 24, 2014, he took N600 million from the office of the former NSA
- Olisa Metuh, former national publicity secretary: on trial for allegedly collecting N1.4 billion from the office of the former NSA
- Raymond Dokpesi, chairman of DAAR Communications: on trial for allegedly taking N2.1 billion from the office of the former NSA
- Dudafa Waripamo-Owei, former SSA to President Goodluck Jonathan: on trial for allegedly keeping over N830 million in accounts of four different companies
- Robert Azibaola, cousin to former President Goodluck Jonathan: allegedly collected $40 million from the office of the former NSA[14]

When releasing the list of the second batch of alleged looters, Mohammed said that those complaining that the first list was too short apparently did not understand that it was strategically released as a teaser.[15] As reported by Premium Times, here is the list of people with the amounts they allegedly embezzled:

- Former NSA Sambo Dasuki: Based on EFCC findings (this is besides the ongoing $2.1 billion military equipment scandal), a total of N126 billion was embezzled through his office. Some of the money was simply shared to people and companies without any formal contract awards.

- Former Petroleum Resources Minister Diezani Alison-Madueke: In just one of the cases the EFCC is investigating, she is alleged to have embezzled about N23 billion. She is also involved in the Strategic Alliance Contracts of the NNPC, where the firms of Jide Omokore and Kola Aluko got oil blocks but never paid government taxes or royalties. About $3 billion was involved. The federal government is charging Omokore and Aluko and will use all legal instruments, local and international, to ensure justice.
- Rtd. Lt.-Gen. Kenneth Minimah: N13.9 billion.
- Lt.-Gen. Azubuike Ihejirika: N4.5 billion.
- Alex Badeh, former Chief of Defence Staff: N8 billion.
- Inde Dikko, former CG of Customs: N40 billion.
- Air Marshal Adesola Amosun: N21.4 billion.
- Senator Bala Abdulkadir Mohammed, former FCT Minister: N5 billion.
- Senator Stella Oduah: N9.8 billion.
- Mu'azu Babangida Aliyu, former governor of Niger State: N1.6 billion – from NSA.
- Senator Jonah Jang, former governor of Plateau State: N12.5 billion.
- Bashir Yuguda, former Minister of State for Finance: N1.5 billion.
- Senator Peter Nwaoboshi: N1.5 billion
- Aliyu Usman, aide to former NSA Dasuki: N512 million
- Ahmad Idris, PA to former NSA Dasuki: N1.5 billion
- Rasheed Ladoja, former governor of Oyo: N500 million
- Tom Ikimi: N300 million
- Femi Fani-Kayode: N866 million
- Hassan Tukur, former PPS to President Goodluck: $1.7

million
- Nenadi Usman: N1.5 billion
- Benedicta Iroha: N1.7 billion
- Aliyu Usman Jawaz, close ally of former NSA Dasuki: N882 million
- Godknows Igali: over N7 billion.[16]

The extent to which public funds in Nigeria have been looted is still difficult to establish. The privileged few continue to sack the treasuries on a daily basis, leaving the common majority in the mess of untold hardship. Kleptocracy has long taken the place of democracy. As lamented by The Nation commentator Tahir Ibrahim Tahir, Nigeria has "a corrupt system of government that has been sustained by selfish individuals who have enriched themselves more than the state itself; and continue to do so, placing their disciples in leadership and other sensitive offices that sustain their game of self-aggrandizement to the detriment of the greater majority."[17] He regrets that most Nigerians have supported this system like a tailwind, urging it on with everyone scrambling for their share of the largesse and providing cover for criminality.[18]

CHAPTER TWO

The Foundation and Evolution Of Nigeria's Corruption

Corruption in Nigeria is not a phenomenon that has mushroomed in contemporary times. It originated even before colonization, playing its role in the British occupation of Nigeria. From that point, it evolved into a monster.

Corruption In Pre-Colonial Days

Before European colonization, corruption existed among the ethnic ruling elites in places that constituted what is now called Nigeria. Scholars such as Philip Curtin and John Fage believed that slave trade was a major factor in the introduction of Africa into the world economy.[1] As evil as slave trade was during pre-colonial times, Curtin asserted that it gave Africans a more developed commercial system, more intense contact with the outer world, and better preparation for dealing with European impact and the challenge of modernization.[2] Similarly, Fage notes that in West Africa, slave trade was part of a sustained process of economic and political development.[3] As debatable as these ideas might be, it is quite certain that Africans were exchanged for rum, gin, clothes, and the like.

The wealth that was so evident in the states of the Niger Delta was created by the people's participation in the slave trade.[4] Nigerian ruling elites manipulated the economic system in a bid to recruit more slaves and make more gains, a vexing example of early corruption.

It is important to understand that African religious institutions in pre-colonial times regulated political, economic, and socio-cultural roles in society. Hence, people's political lives had no clear distinction from their religious lives.[5] Therefore, religious institutions played a major role in the economics and politics of the slave trade. For instance, in the southeastern part of Nigeria, the Aro sought to establish their hegemony by manipulating the dominant role of their god, the Long Juju, to get slaves.[6] In the absence of a large-scale state structure in that area, the Aro god emerged as the major arbiter in disputes between communities that had no other machinery for solving them.[7] Social offenders like those who committed incest or broke traditional taboo, plus criminal offenders like murderers, were sold.[8] Okon Uya points out that before maturation of the slave trade, such disputants paid fines in goods and services to the Aro priests, but in the slave trade era, the Aro insisted on fines being paid in slaves.[9] According to Kenneth Dike, by manipulating the influence of their Long Juju-god, the Aro came to dominate slave recruitment in the southeastern section of Nigeria.[10]

Pre-colonial Nigerians used other corrupt means to recruit slaves as well. Some, especially strangers, were kidnapped as slave raids were organized by stronger states against their weaker neighbors.[11] The extent of this profit motive was overtly demonstrated during the campaign to suppress the slave trade. Some rulers of Old Calabar and Kosoko of Lagos, among others, dismissed British efforts to stop the trade as madness emanating from European foolishness.[12] The rulers did not want to stop selling their own kind. They enriched themselves by sending members of their population to Europe and to the Americas, though the manpower they were exporting was needed for the agriculture that served as the mainstay of the economy at the time. This is similar to rulers' present-day mindsets, when it's okay to loot and stash money that could otherwise serve as capital for domestic economic development.

Even after the British outlawed overseas slave trade in 1807, the trade in humans continued. For this reason, the British campaigned for other European nations, America, and participating African chiefs to end the business.[13] Nigerians chiefs in particular were lured into signing treaties negotiated by the British. Such treaties were signed in Brass in 1834, Bonny in 1839, Calabar in 1841 and Aboh in 1842.[14] Under their provisions, the rulers of pre-colonial

Nigerian states were to be compensated over an agreed-upon number of years for giving up the trade in slaves. The importance of these treaties was that once signed, the British used them as an excuse to bombard Nigerian states on the pretext that some articles of them had been violated.[15] Because of the proclivity of some corrupt chiefs to wage double deals, they inadvertently invited British intrusion into their domains, forcing their communities to accept the superiority of Britain. According to Obaro Ikime, "it is clear, therefore, that in retrospect, the suppression of the overseas slave trade provided an indispensable prelude to the British occupation of Nigeria.[16]

Corruption In Colonial Times

Ghanaian nationalist and former President Kwame Nkrumah was of the opinion that the impact of Western culture on the African mind brought as much bad as good in its trail,[17] citing European encroachment as a huge reason for corruption. A handful of scholars offered another opinion, that corruption was introduced into Nigeria by freed slaves brought from Sierra Leone by British colonialists. When they (Sierra Leoneans) came, B.E. Umoh explains that,

> *"They were able to understand the English Language, which Nigerians did not understand. When the British colonial regime commenced, its officials made them as interpreters, chief clerks, heads of police departments and so forth. They were also the first lawyers and business middlemen. They had access to the kings, and thus were something of a go-between for Europeans and the African potentates. They took advantage of the situation by initiating a system of bribery never known in the Nigerian political history."[18]*

It should be noted that the colony of Sierra Leone, inspired by humanitarian opposition to slavery and nurtured by British determination to end slave trade in West Africa, was founded in 1787 with groups of black settlers from England, Nova Scotia, and Jamaica. Freetown, its capital, was made headquarters of the British Naval Squadron in West Africa, who were charged with the responsibility of averting further export of slaves across the Atlantic. Over time the colony evolved, and by 1850 about 40,000 ex-slaves had settled there.[19] The recaptured slaves evolved into a distinct group known as the Creole. Western education developed in the colony and the first school, Fourah Bay College, was established in 1876.[20] The system produced many educated persons. Necessity made the Creoles adventurous,[21] and the Creoles of Sierra Leone occupied lucrative subordinate positions of trust in both the military and the civil service of government in four coastal colonies and settlements: Sierra Leone, the Gambia, the Gold Coast, and Lagos. They also settled in Abeokuta, the Niger, Bonny, and Old Calabar.[22]

The Sierra Leoneans were also partners in the despicable crime of introducing corruption to Nigeria. To gain some advantage over their European competitors, these merchants offered chiefs money, gifts, and foreign or funny titles and names.[23] Ayandele noted that Sierra Leoneans "flattered the chiefs with frequent visits and patronized the king's regular banquets."[24]

As colonialism evolved, the Nigerian economy became monetized in 1906 and capitalism began to take its toll on the social formations of various communities.[25] It should be noted that in capitalism, the individual acquisition of wealth is the index of success, and one's importance is not determined by ancestry or birthright, but by what a person can acquire. At the early stage in Nigeria, corruption was minimal, but with the monetization of the economy, rulers and citizens started to chase both money and the power it bestowed.[26]

The colonial masters, in tandem, used money and power to prop up rulers who did their bidding. Rulers, who would normally be ejected by their constituents at the hint of corruption, became untouchable. The masses came to realize that leadership at all levels was backed by money and power and was beyond their control. This system transcended the colonial era, and unfortunately remains the modus operandi of the post-colonial political system.[27]

Later in the colonial era, educated Nigerians were compelled to occupy positions earlier held by British officers, working at marketing boards established at the three regions. According to Agedah, huge sums of money accrued as a result of underpayment to palm oil, cocoa, and groundnut farmers were mismanaged by the political class.[28]

Instances of corruption in Nigeria during the colonial period abound. One example is when Effiong Okon Eyo, a former government chief whip, leveled serious accusations in 1956 against Dr. Nnamdi Azikiwe, then-Premier of the Eastern Region. He alleged that Azikiwe grossly abused his office when he deposited public funds in the African Continental Bank, a private bank in which he was a principal shareholder.[29] The allegations led to a tribunal of enquiry chaired by Sir Stafford Foster Sutton, Chief Justice of Nigeria, which reportedly sat for 50 days. After deliberation, it concluded that

> *"Dr. Azikiwe's primary motive was to make available an indigenous bank with the object of liberalizing credit to the people of this country, but we are satisfied that he was attracted by the financial powers his interest in the bank gave him… we consider his conduct in the matter has fallen short of the expectations of honest, reasonable people."[30]*

In 1955, when the Eastern Regional Government set up a commission of inquiry to investigate the extent of bribery and corruption, there were two cases: one involving M.C. Agwu, regional Minister of Lands, who was accused of impropriety in the allocation of urban plots, and one involving the Minister of Finance, Mazi Mbonu Ojike, who was linked to corruption at the time he was serving as the Minister of Public Works.[31] The latter allegation had to do with the construction of the famous Onitsha market, estimated to have cost £433,000. The claim was that Ojike exerted his influence to award the contract to a firm called Borini Prono and Company, for which he would be paid one shilling on every pound of the contract value. The accuser, who complained that he was not paid, was said to have been promised one penny on every shilling. The chairman of a three-man commission of inquiry declared publicly that Mazi Ojike was indeed corrupt. Premier Azikiwe eventually asked him to resign.[32]

There was another case that involved the indictment and subsequent removal from office of Alhaji Adegoke Adelabu as the Chairman of the Ibadan District Council in 1956. At the time, Adelabu doubled as a minister in the federal cabinct, but was compelled to resign after being found culpable of corruption and maladministration charges.[33]

In yet another example, a commission of inquiry in the Western Region was set up in the last decade of the colonial period to ascertain the verity of allegations of financial impropriety leveled against the Nigerian political party Action Group under the leadership of Chief Obafemi Awolowo. A witness during the probe testified that the Action Group operated a company for which Awolowo was the sole holder, and that he used the Nigeria Investment Promotion Commission (NIPC) to create a financial empire of which he was the head.[34] According to findings, between April 1958 and November 1962, the Action Group-led government of Western Nigeria invested £6,500,000 of public funds in the NIPC.[35] Although the commission concluded that Chief Awolowo did not aspire to personally enrich himself, the same could not be said of his lieutenants. The Cooker Commission discovered that loans granted to NIPC ended up in the pockets of some of its directors.[36]

Corruption in the Post-Colonial Times

The First Republic was Nigeria's first period of government under a republican constitution, but it was also a watershed of corruption in Nigeria's political history: bribes were demanded, contracts inflated, mobilization fees were collected on contract projects that were never executed, and politicians were known to privately acquire and accumulate state resources.[37] One of the major reasons the Nigerian army, led by Major Chukwuma Kaduna Nzeogwu, aborted the First Republic on January 15, 1966 was because of infractions bordering on corruption. In his maiden broadcast, Nzeogwu declared

> *"Our enemies are political profiteers, the swindlers, the men in high and low places that seek bribes and demand 10%... Those that have corrupted our society and put the Nigerian political calendar back by their words and deeds."[38]*

From January 15, 1966 when the first coup d'etat took place, the military ruled until 1999. An early attempt by the military government to combat corruption was unsuccessful, as subsequent military regimes fully embraced corruption and entrenched it in every fabric of national life.

It should be noted that that first military coup paved the way for General Aguiyi Ironsi's regime, who only ruled the country for six months before he was assassinated on July 29, 1966. General Yakubu Gowon then took power, and his government lasted until

July 29, 1975. Although there were no significant accusations of corruption trailing him personally, there were brazen cases perpetrated under his watch. General Gowon did promise that new measures would be introduced to make those found guilty of corruption disgorge their ill-gotten gains, and that special tribunals would be set up to deal speedily with corruption in all organs of public service.[39]

Corruption, however, continued unabated under Gowon's administration. One case that really stained his government was the cement scam. According to a Musa Yar'Adua Foundation report, "What started as a bottleneck was caused principally by massive ordering of cement by the army intending to build barracks for soldiers after the Nigerian Civil War. Thirteen million tons of cement at a cost of 960 million dollars, and an additional four million tons ordered by the Ministry of Works caused problems that sparked a scam, as vessels parked themselves in the Atlantic Ocean demanding demurrage payments that reached the then extraordinary sum of 1 million Naira per day for cargoes that were sometimes non-existent or for orders that had never been placed. Beyond the creeks and channels surrounding Lagos, hundreds of ships littered the horizon, a symbol of the inertia and corruption of the Gowon regime."[40]

The regime was weak in the fight against corruption. On one occasion, the press and the public had to pressure Joseph Tarka, the Federal Commissioner of Communication, to resign[41] following allegations that he owned and operated a coded Swiss bank account while also co-owning Nigeria Investment Quest Limited. His private secretary S. Ikowe served as managing director, and the company was used in trades with the Ministry of Communication where he (Tarka) served as commissioner.[42] When Generals Murtala Mohammed and Olusegun Obasanjo's administrations succeeded Gowon's, several tribunals were set up to unravel circumstances of corruption of the previous regime. At the end of the day, out of 11 governors and one administrator, only Brigadier Mobolaji Johnson of Lagos State and Brigadier Oluwole Rotimi of Western State were absolved of corruption.[43] The total value of assets confiscated following the investigations was worth more than N10,000,000.

During the regimes of Mohammed and Obasanjo, there were cases of corrupt practices leveled against officials of the administration, but they were not as pronounced as what happened under Gowon.[44]

Corruption under President Shehu Shagari (1979-1983), however, rose to an alarming level of incidence and magnitude. There was immense availability of funds owing to the oil boom of the 1970s, but it was claimed that over $16 billion in oil revenues were lost during Shegari's regime.[45] At the same time, Transport Minister Alhaji Umaru Dikko was alleged to have mismanaged about $4 billion in public funds meant for the importation of rice.[46] This gives context to the infamous Dikko Affair in 1984, when Umaru Dikko was kidnapped in London and transported via container to Nigeria in order to stand for a corruption case during General Muhammadu Buhari's regime.

It became quite common during Shagari's administration for federal buildings to mysteriously go up in flames, most especially just before the onset of audits of government accounts, making it impossible to discover written evidence of embezzlement and fraud.[47] When Buhari took power from Shagari, his house-cleansing crusade led to the imprisonment of several public officials on charges of malpractice and looting of public funds.

After a palace coup that ousted Buhari in August of 1985, General Ibrahim Babangida came into power. Corruption seems to have been a way of life under Babangida, and it was elevated almost to state policy during that period.[48] The American magazine The

Enquirer reported that "roughly, 3,000 officials had Swiss Bank accounts totaling $33 billion.[49]

Babangida's administration eventually set up a panel of enquiry to investigate the operation of the Central Bank of Nigeria (CBN), and the report submitted in 1994 showed that the CBN could not account for 12.1 billion dollars received from the oil sales in 1991.[50] Uwem Akpan, quoting a confidential report published in December 1993, noted that the Babangida government squandered the $12.4 billion windfall that the country made during the Gulf Crisis in 1991. The London Financial Times reported that at least $3 billion of the estimated $5 billion that Nigeria earned from the Gulf Crisis was unaccounted for in the CBN's report. As a result of this revelation, the Financial Times reporter was deported from Nigeria on the pretext that he was misleading the public.[51]

T.T. Mamadu, quoting The Financial Times and The News, enumerated various cases of mismanagement and corrupt practices under Babangida's regime as follows:

- 12 billion dollars Gulf Crisis windfall in 1991
- 30 percent of oil revenue annually diverted to frivolous uses
- Huge extra budgetary spending: 1989 – N15.3 billion; 1990 – N23.4 billion; 1991 – N35 billion; 1992 – N44.2 billion; and 1993 - N59 billion (by August)
- 200 million dollars siphoned from the Aluminum Smelter project
- N400 million wasted on the Better Life Project
- Colossal corruption at the NNPC (example: questionable contracts of N101 million for the purchases of Strategic Storage Facilities)[52]

General Sani Abacha's reign (1993-1998) was at best the zenith of corruption in Nigeria. According to Professor Okon Eminue,

Abacha's kleptomaniac propensity for financial misappropriation was legendary.[53] He, his family, and his associates were estimated to have looted $3 billion to $5 billion of public assets, transferring much of this money abroad.[54] A report attributed to the Swiss Federal Banking Commission has it that 19 banks had dealings with Abacha's regime.[55]

> *"The money looted from the treasury by Abacha," reports Nigerian columnist Olusegun Adeniyi, "was amassed by awarding contracts to front companies, accepting massive bribes and by siphoning money directly from the Nigerian treasury. There were indeed tales, most of it now confirmed, of crooked oil deals, debt buy-back scams and vans delivering stacks of bank notes, in local and foreign currencies, from the Central Bank to the homes of Abacha's family members and cronies."[56]*

Victor Onyeka-Ben reported that the money recovered from the Abacha family became possible through assistance provided by former National Security Adviser Alhaji Ismaila Gwarzo, who consistently maintained that he was just an errand boy in the pillage of the state treasury.[57] Later, however, Gwarzo admitted to owning properties and vehicles that the federal government confiscated. These included 28 houses in Abuja, five in Zaria, three in Kano and one in Gwarzo village, all worth some billions of naira. He was also found in possession of 16 trailers loaded with fertilizer, though when investigated, he claimed that 10 of the trailers and fertilizers belonged to the late Abacha. In addition, Gwarzo reportedly forfeited $128 million worth of shares in, among others, the West African Refineries in Sierra Leone.[58]

Although the government of General Abdulsalami Abubakar, who succeeded Abacha, indicated commitment to returning the country to democracy, the regime was implicated by a contract review panel a week after Obasanjo assumed office as president.[59] "General Abubakar spent the last five months of his tenure decapitating the country while maintaining an incredibly innocent man," reported Eminue. "The regime had frittered away Nigeria's 2.3 billion Dollars in foreign exchange deal. And, despite a ceiling of 80 billion Naira approved as capital vote for government ministries and parastatals in the 1999 budget, officials of (Abubakar's) government approved and awarded contracts worth over 640 billion Naira within that short period of time before Obasanjo assumed office."[60]

The swearing-in of Chief Olusegun Obasanjo as president ushered in the Fourth Republic on May 29, 1999. There was hope that the democratic government would automatically dissolve the culture of corruption. Unfortunately, the rate of corruption continued to increase and reached alarmingly high levels. Out of 99 total countries investigated for the Corruption Perception Index by Transparency International in 1999, Nigeria emerged as the second most corrupt with a score of 1.6. The country was topped only by Cameroon, its West African neighbor, with a score of 1.5. Consistently afterwards, Nigeria has been a member of the infamous club of most corrupt countries in the world.[61] For more on cases of corruption since 1999, see chapter four.

Nigeria has a problem that breeds corruption: the enthronement and glorification of materialism. From pre-colonial to contemporary times, the love for materialistic prosperity seems to preoccupy societal desires. If material acquisition is the root cause of evil, injustice, oppression, and inhumanity, as M.A. Fashona asserts,[62] it therefore seems that the situation that enables Nigeria's wanton corruption is entrenched in materialistic greed.

by Dr. Darlington Akaiso

CHAPTER THREE

The Eleventh Player: A Soccer Approach

In soccer, coaches strategize around team formations. A formation could be a traditional 4-4-2, or it may be 4-3-3; some coaches go for 4-1-4-1, some for 4-5-1. Others choose the 3-5-2 currently in vogue. The common denominator is that they are all made up of ten players. But in soccer, a side's standard number of players is 11.

So why is the eleventh player missing?

In a lineup consisting of 11 players, there are ten outfield players and one goal-keeper, the latter of whom is not captured in the formation. While the ten other players wear similar colors and kits, the goal-keeper sports a different jersey with a different color. While rules prevent the other ten players from using their hands, the goalie has no such restrictions. He is the eleventh player, and he follows his own set of rules.

In Nigerian politics, it is much the same. There are outfield players who appear officially in the government's formation, but other important players lie totally outside of that. Those visible politicians are the ones incumbent: the president, vice president, secretary to the federation, ministers, commissioners, governors, deputy governors, legislators, justices, service chiefs, personnel of MDAs, local government council members, and all other political appointees.

The metaphorical eleventh players - just as influential but playing by a different set of rules - are spouses, family members, sexual partners, and acolytes of political office holders. They are political godfathers, bank staffers, contractors, religious fathers, party members, security personnel, career civil servants, voters, international actors, media practitioners, academics, lawyers, estate managers, thugs, and businessmen who associate in one way or the other with the serving politicians. The list could be endless, but the bottom line is that any association with a politician has the potential to corrupt. What makes corruption thrive are the complementary roles played by the visible and by those behind the scenes.

It is through competitive quest for material wealth that Nigerians see the resources of the country as the cake meant for individual self-enrichment. To compete for their own cake, they coalesce into teams. They push themselves into power positions in order to have a share of the booty. As networks or syndicates, they delegate roles in their struggle for power, ensuring that some of their own are active in the system while others play their roles in the background.

In the process of government formation, key supporters see the candidate as a project, a contact point through whom they can access state wealth.

The eleventh player on a political team consists of actors who are not holding office but are nevertheless part of the game. The first set of these actors are the godfathers who are powerbrokers in Nigerian politics. They are rich and influential. They invest their money in candidates, assuring them of assistance in exchange for personal benefit.[1] When their clients win elections, the godfathers look to the agreements reached pre-election. They feel entitled to a certain number of slots in which to insert political appointees; they demand employment favors, contracts, and land allocations. Most of all, the godfathers expect state money paid on a monthly basis. Indeed, it is this unjustified demand for allocation of state financial resources that boosts crass looting of state funds.

As said by Isaac Olawale Albert,

"the relationship between political godfathers and their adopted sons is usually transactional in nature: it is a case of 'you rub my back, and I rub your back', as Nigerians say. Like every businessmen, godfathers invest in their 'grandsons' and expect returns after elections."[2]

A clear example of how a godfather can influence his godson in power is the case between Chief Chris Uba and Chris Ngige. When Uba, an iconic figure in Anambra politics, decided to raise his own candidate for the governorship position in 2003, he settled for Chris Ngige, a medical practitioner, whom he thought would be amenable. The two agreed to work together, and Uba assured his candidate of victory, bargaining hard.[3] Part of the agreement reached with Ngige was that Uba would get seven of the ten commissioner positions in the state if Ngige win the election, and that Uba could identify the juicy ministries to be manned by his commissioners.[4]

Ngige did win the 2003 gubernatorial election, and Uba, his godfather, declared:

> *"I am the greatest of all godfathers in Nigeria. Because this is the first time one single individual has single-handedly put in position every politician in a state: the State Governor and his deputy; the 3 Senators to represent the State at the National Assembly; 10 out of 11 members of the Federal House of Reps; twenty-nine State House of Assembly members; I also have the power to remove any of them who does not perform up to my expectations anytime I like."[5]*

This illustrates that sometimes, political office holders are mere outfield players captained by one playing by a whole other set of rules. The eleventh man exerts more influence than the outfield ten, and it is a major factor in corruption. Ngige, following a fallout with Uba, later exposed thus:

> *"Chris Uba took my former accountant-general into his hotel room in Abuja at NICON. And they typed a letter to*

the Central Bank of Nigeria, CBN, opening up an Irrevocable Standing Payment Order, ISPO, on his project that has been on before then. He told me that Dr Nbadinuju stopped his ISPO because of the political crisis between them. So he called me to sign this document directing the Central Bank to pay him from the federation account N10 million monthly for the next 87 months totaling N870 million. I said I could not do that for two reasons: First and foremost, I would not be in office for 87 months. I will only be governor for 48 months that is four years. That if I will ever sign an IPSO, it is for 48 months. Secondly, there are no accompanying certificates to prove or show that you are entitled to N870 million. Thirdly, it is wrong for you to bring my accountant-general into a hotel room with a prepared letter by him and yourself and you expect me to sign it for you. He did not like it. He started making trouble ... Again, he said his election expenses total N3 billion and that he wanted a cheque from me. I told him that nobody can give a cheque of N3 billion. He insisted I should also sign an agreement. But I asked, 'how did you come about the N3 billion?' He flared up.[6]*

This political office holder was expected to please his background backer by dipping his hand in the coffers of the state. This type of expectation breeds corruption. A breach of agreement by the political godson can easily lead to a serious political disturbance, as is exactly what happened in Anambra post-fallout between Uba and Ngige. The result threw the state into chaos, whereby lives were endangered and properties destroyed.

Political jobbers also put tremendous pressure on the political ruling class. These people live on politics. They are often not as rich as their clients, but they are well-versed in the manipulation necessary to win elections at the grassroots level. They are familiar with the formal and informal ways to win over constituencies[7] and can use that to leverage payments from the candidate. They are given slots, direct appointments, monetary rewards, and sometimes juicy contracts. Most of these politician-turned-contractors end up embezzling project funds and get off scot-free.

Another influential factor in Nigeria's corruption narrative is the interrelationship between corporations and political actors. Companies play a major role in the implementation of capital projects. Some companies flout the contract award procedures and circumvent bidding processes to bribe appropriate and influential politicians. Note that these companies are not part of the state political system, but their role in perpetuating political corruption seems enormous. The $180 million Halliburton bribe scandal offers a suitable example here.

In 1994, M.W. Kellogg, a subsidiary of Halliburton, formed a partnership called TSKJ with Technip of France, Snamprogetti of the Netherlands, and Japan Gasoline Corp, submitting a bid to Nigeria's Liquefied Natural Gas (NLNG). TSKJ bid $2 billion for the contract, but it was not immediately accepted even though it was 5% lower than that of a co-competitor. It allegedly took a series of bribes to pave the way for TSKJ to emerge as the favored contractor.[8]

Halliburton, in a statement following the deal, announced that the Nigerian government had awarded a $1.2 billion contract to TSKJ to expand the construction of the natural gas plant from two trains to three trains in order to increase the plant's capacity by 50 percent. According to a document obtained by The Nation, those implicated in the bribery scandal included four ex-heads of state, two former chiefs of general staff, two ex-first ladies, the ex-CBN governor, three former military governors or administrators, a former deputy governor of CBN, 11 former ministers (including two ex-ministers of petroleum resources), two retired permanent secretaries, and three ex-NNPC GMDs.

There were many others involved as well: ex-secretaries to the government of the federation, a former civilian governor, a former ambassador to Italy, an ex-envoy to Brazil, three ex-NNPC secretaries, a former chief security officer to a former head of state… the list goes on.[9]

Then-chairman of Kellogg Brown & Root and consultant for Halliburton Albert J. Stanley later admitted in court that he orchestrated more than $180 million in bribes to senior government officials, adding that they were channeled through a UK-based lawyer in four multi-million dollar installments.[10] The bribe was allegedly facilitated between 1995 and 2005 in London.[11]

The Malabu oil scandal is another example of a political and corporate partnership for corruption. Dan Etete, former Minister of Petroleum, set himself up with Malabu Oil and Gas, a company reportedly incorporated in five days before the oil block was awarded to it during the regime Sani Abacha.[12] While trying to cover his link to the company, Etete registered the company with a fictitious director, Kweku Amafegha, and the company went on to list a fake address in registration documents.[13] More than half of the N171.32 billion paid to Malabu Oil and Gas for the procurement of one of Nigeria's richest oil fields was used to bribe Nigerian politicians and intermediaries who helped secure the controversial deal.[14] Etete confessed to a British court in 2013 that former President Olusegun Obasanjo demanded a slice of the oil block as a bribe.[15]

Spouses, children, siblings, relatives, sex partners and friends of political leaders are also among the corrupt. These appendages hurriedly set up private companies when their benefactors take power, and convert them as veritable tools to rip off the state-held financial resources. This scenario is commonplace in Nigeria today.

One notable example is the case in which the Federal High Court in Kano ordered an interim forfeiture of N1 billion traced to Magel Resort Limited, a company linked to Dame Patience Jonathan, wife of former president Goodluck Jonathan.[16] According to The Nation, the former first lady and other relatives were directors of the company.[17]

As acting head of media and publicity of the EFCC, Tony Orilade released this statement in February of 2019: "The Commission had received an intelligence that a bank account domiciled in Fidelity Bank, had a huge sum of money that was not being used by anybody. Upon receipt of the intelligence, the EFCC swung into action by conducting a preliminary investigation, which revealed that Patience and some relatives of former president, Goodluck Jonathan, were directors of the company.

> *"In trying to trace the origin of the money, it was discovered that N500,000 was deposited on the 20th May, 2015 by Fynface, who is alleged to be in charge of the company, while N1 billion was transferred in two tranches on the 25th May, 2015 from PAGMAT Oil and Gas Nigeria Limited, a company that was not incorporated with Corporate Affairs Commission."*[18]

Companies mostly serve as ready tools in the hands of the corrupt. They often are used to manipulate the system and drain national resources for private use. In 2012, for example, fraudulent dealings in the oil subsidy program were alleged to have been perpetrated by companies that were importing refined petroleum products into Nigeria. According to Dr. Ngozi Okonjo-Iweala, "these fraudulent dealings went beyond the smuggling of oil shipments over the border into neighboring countries such as Benin and Niger, where prices were much higher. Allegations were rife that companies were claiming subsidies for shipments of oil never delivered. For shipments of kerosene, allegations swirled that corrupt payments were being made to assign the rights to import cargos of subsidized kerosene to certain companies, which then sold the kerosene to consumers at nonsubsidized prices."[19]

To investigate these allegations, an ad-hoc committee to verify and determine the actual subsidy requirement was set up by the House of Representatives in January 2012. Some companies then demonstrated how the corrupt could try to fight back. Zenon Oil and Gas Ltd and Synopsis Enterprises Ltd, belonging to Nigerian billionaire businessman Femi Otedola, were two of the oil marketing companies on a list for sanctions for receiving millions of dollars in foreign exchange for oil imports they didn't make.[20] A leaked video showed that the chairman of the ad-hoc committee, Hon. Farouk Lawan, purportedly received a large bribe from Otedola to help expunge the two companies from the list. As explained by Okonjo-Iweala, "the brouhaha about the bribery scandal quickly eclipsed discussion of the report and its findings."[21]

The Nation reported another incident in December 2019: Stephen Amase, private secretary to the Benue State governor, and Emmanuel Manger, the former state commissioner for work, used their positions to perpetrate a N4.7 billion contract scam through Tongyi New International Construction Limited.[22] Rasheedat Okoduwa, spokesperson for Independent Corrupt Practices and Other Related Offenses (ICPC), reacted before the Benue State High Court: "the suspects were arraigned for conferring unfair advantage upon themselves and for holding indirect private interest in a contract valued at N4,766,858,449.63."[23]

Communities also play an important role as eleventh man on metaphorical Team Corruption. Members of the community from which a politician hails can become vexatious background players who encourage them to go neck deep in the practices of the corrupt. The value system has become so warped that political leaders are now openly pressurized to indulge in blatant corruption. Citing the World Bank write-up, Ngozi Okonjo-Iweala brings these points to fore:

> *"It is important to understand how the decision to engage in corruption takes place in the mind of a public official. If people believe that the purpose of obtaining office is to provide one's family and friends with money, goods, favors, or appointments, then social networks can perpetuate the norm of corruption. Social networks can even serve as a source of punishment for public servants who violate that norm… Holders of public positions who did not use their influence to assist friends and relatives risked derision and disrespect."[24]*

In Nigeria, it can be astonishing to see how many members of a community express solidarity with a political kinsman accused of corrupt practices. In fact, James Ibori, the former governor of Delta State, was given a heroic welcome following his arrival in the country in February 2017 after serving a jail term in the United Kingdom over charges bordering on corruption and money laundering. According to a news report, "Oghara, the capital of Ethiope East Local Government Area, had been electrified since the people got wind of Ibori's imminent return following his release from prison last December 21. The town was agog with jubilation as the crowd of kinsmen and associates of the former governor sang and danced from Oghara junction, along the Warri-Benin expressway, where they had waited for him, to his country house. The crowds erupted into a loud and long session of praise songs and prayers as the convoy entered the palatial compound."[25]

Something similar happened in 2005 when Diepreye Alamieyeseigha, who was serving as the governor of Bayelsa

State, returned to his home village a folk hero after apparently escaping Europe in a dress and on a forged passport. Crowds cheered and waved to welcome him back and This Day published a photo montage of him in a red dress, necklace, head-dress and lipstick. "Today I am back at my desk, forever committed to serve the people of Bayelsa and Nigeria. I thank the almighty God for his protection," said Alamieyeseigha to his kinsmen.[26] The governor was arrested at Heathrow Airport in September 2005, had his passport confiscated, and faced three money-laundering charges after police found £1 million in cash at his London address and property in his name worth £10m.[27]

CHAPTER FOUR

Themes In Nigeria's Corruption Narrative Since 1999

On May 29, 2016, in a special edition marking the 17th anniversary of Nigeria's democracy, The Punch Newspaper reported that the country had lost more than N38 trillion through mismanagement, embezzlement, and money laundering under successive administrations since democracy returned in 1999.[1] The newspaper said the figures were drawn from findings by anti-graft agencies and investigative panel reports on major economic scandals and financial crimes in the country, pointing out that the investigations, which covered the Obasanjo, Yar'Adua, and Jonathan administrations, showed that most of the stolen funds have not been accounted for.[2]

In the years since that article was published, it has become apparent that the amount of resources lost to official sleaze far exceeds N38 trillion. Even with Muhammadu Buhari's administration's anti-corruption effort, there is no certainty that the amount of looting has scaled down. The highly celebrated democracy that returned in 1999 is one in name only, as its so-called dividends are increasingly being frittered away by the minority in power. As Tochukwu Ezukanma rightfully noted, the problem of Nigeria's democracy is that, like in a dictatorship, the powers of the governing are not subject to the will of the governed. He laments that Nigeria remains a dictatorship with merely the façade of democracy.[3]

Nigeria's democracy does not just tend toward dictatorship; it has become apparent that kleptocracy has emerged, an umbrella under which those in power commandeer and siphon national wealth while the majority languish in poverty. The following pages highlight selected financial scandals that have rocked Nigeria since 1999.

Obasanjo Administration (1999-2007)

When democracy was ushered in on May 29, 1999, the people

expected the civilian government to show fiscal discipline and responsibility. The budgets in the eight years of Obasanjo were hardly carried through, however, with the best of them eliciting only 35% implementation.[4] You can see from the cases of corruption outlined below that Obasanjo's government laid a grand foundation for corruption to thrive.

A $16 Billion Power Sector Scandal

At the beginning of Chief Olusegun Obasanjo's administration in 1999, he promised to ensure an adequate and affordable power supply given the primacy of electricity in the growth and sustainability of the economy as well as the general development of society. Thus, the National Electric Power Authority (NEPA) was unbundled and was succeeded by the Power Holding Company. On January 31, 2008, the House of Representatives charged a committee to look into how much was spent on power projects, and the ensuing report clearly establishes that "the total expenditure in the power sector during the period 1999-2007 was US $13,278,937,409.94."[5] The report further points out that "had the supplementary budget of the power sector in 2007 been implemented, the expenditure could then have been over $16 billion".[6] During Obasanjo's administration, the power sector served as one of the numerous bottomless cesspits through which public funds disappeared. Power supply continues to remain epileptic. Although the monumental corruption was duly investigated by a joint committee of the National Assembly, the report never saw the light of day.[7]

NNPC's Opaque Deals

Scholar Uwem Akpan claims that Chief Olusegun Obasanjo should not be exonerated from the allegations of corruption in the oil sector because he doubled as the President and the Minister of Petroleum, even when he appointed Edmund Daukoru as Minister of State for Energy during his second term.[8] As revealed by the Chairman of Revenue Mobilization Allocation and Fiscal Commission (RMAFC) in August 2007, the Nigerian National Petroleum Corporation (NNPC) withheld a total sum of N560 billion from the federation account between December 2004 and April 2007.[9] Akpan added that "the NNPC does not account for the other products but it also withholds about 20 billion naira every month from the Federation Account as subsidy."[10]

The Hart Group, a UK-based audit firm, found that about 65 million barrels of the crude oil sold between 1999 and 2004 could not be accounted for.[11] In fact, the NNPC in 2000 claimed it sold 54 million barrels of crude oil worth $1.47 billion to Carlson (Bermuda) Limited, while Carlson said that it actually purchased crude oil and petroleum products amounting to $225 billion.[12] Okoi-Uyouyo noted that between 2000 and 2001, the value of petroleum products supplied by Carlson to NNPC was worth $250 million and $205 million respectively, saying that NNPC might have diverted crude oil worth $2 billion between 2000 and 2001 alone.[13]

There was a time in 2001 when crude oil was selling at $35 dollars per barrel in the international market. NNPC was paying $18 per barrel, though, for an excess 300,000 barrels it could not refine. Thus, they were able to make a daily profit of $5,100,000 from these transactions.[14]

There was another bribery scandal surrounding the construction of the Escravos Gas to Liquid (EGTL) project by NNPC. Employees of Willbros Group admitted to making corrupt payments totaling more than $6.3 million to Nigerian government officials for work on the Eastern Gas System, prompting the US Department of Justice to fine the company $22 million.[15]

Oil Blocs Contract Scam

Oil blocs were reportedly used as settlement tools during Obasanjo's administration. Some companies that bid and won had no experience in the oil industry, while some were registered solely for the bids, coming into existence only a few days previous.[16] Eight days prior to the end of Obasanjo's administration, he awarded contracts estimated at N752 billion. Due to the apparent fraudulent nature of these awards, the NNPC board refused to ratify them. This led to Obasanjo sacking the board while ordering the NNPC's group managing director to constitute an ad-hoc committee to process and award contracts in a brazen violation of all rules governing such things.[17] The awards included $753,287,449 to Cameron; $1,790,901,102 to Technip; $1,753,787,687 to Saipem; $969,267,000 to Seadrill; and $537,000,000 to Skillbase.[18]

Missing N300 Billion at Ministry of Works

In 2009, Chief Tony Anenih, Minister of Works during Obasanjo's administration, was indicted by a committee constituted by the National Assembly to investigate how N300 billion went missing during his ministry.[19] The missing money was widely believed to have been used to pay off the 2003 election expenses, and the committee recommended the prosecution of 13 former ministers, including Anenih, because they allegedly awarded contracts without budgetary provisions.[20]

Bode George and the NPA Scandal

A special committee headed by Nuhu Ribadu to investigate the board and management of the Nigerian Port Authority (NPA) from 2001 to 2003 described the port authority "as one of the parastatals where irregularities and malpractices have become deeply entrenched."[21] It was discovered that the NPA, under the chairmanship of Chief Olubode George, had approved various contracts in clear violation of extant laws. The contracts were said to have numbered over 24,000 and valued at more than N100 billion.[22] These contracts were generally inflated, not budgeted for, and resulted in the NPA accumulating a huge contract debt running into billions of naira without corresponding value, and Olubode George was investigated by the EFCC and sentenced to years of imprisonment on account of corruption and abuse of office.[23]

Aviation Scandals

The aviation sector during Obasanjo's administration was another cesspool of corruption. Numerous scandals include the N6.5 billion Safe Tower contract which was inflated by N4.5 billion; the missing N300 million earmarked for severance pay for sacked workers of the Federal Aviation Authority of Nigeria (FAAN); and N1.7 billion paid to "ghost" contractors of FAAN.[24]

Rail System Project Fund Mismanagement

About N33 billion was initially awarded to the China Civil Engineering Construction Company for work on a rail system, but it was allegedly mismanaged. The project was expected to commence in 2006 under a 25-year program, but it did not take off during Obasanjo's administration. Payment was reportedly made for the first phase of the standard gauge line spanning over 1,315km from Lagos to Kano.[25]

Mismanagement of the PTDF

Both President Obasanjo and Vice President Atiku Abubakar were linked to the diversion of money from the Petroleum Development Fund (PTDF) to their own private use. There were allegations of a total lack of checks and balances in the fund disbursement, which was mired by an opacity of transactions. Besides the allegations against the president and his deputy, there was also a long list of people called up for interrogation.

In the initial response to the allegations, Garba Shehu, media consultant to the vice president, made reference to a statement to the EFCC made by Otunba Samuel Oyewole Fasawe. Fasawe was a businessman and friend to Atiku and Obasanjo, and he identified a special assistant to Obasanjo as a conduit through which money reached him.[26] Shehu alleged that a total of N3 billion went to Obasanjo from another account run by Fasawe.[27] The audit report subsequently listed Adeyanju as the recipient of N17 million.[28]

The audit report also accused Vice President Atiku Abubakar for unilaterally approving the release of an additional $20 million to PTDF without approval of the Federal Executive Council, though he attempted a satisfactory explanation.[29] Both the audit report and that of the EFCC agreed that Fasawe and his companies had a long-standing relationship with the vice president, tracing local drafts worth N61 million and N250 million to Abubakar and Marine Float Limited. Both reports also said that the vice president was connected to a Marine Float account at Bank PHB, through which "several suspicious transactions in hundreds of millions of naira" passed.[30]

There were a lot of corrupt practices reported by the auditors on PTDF. For instance, a contract was signed in June 2001 between PTDF and Univation Limited in the United Kingdom for the supervision of the upgrade of the Petroleum Training Institute (PTI) in Delta State. According to SaharaReporters, "Out of the $5.35 million paid Univation as mobilization and set-up fee for the PTI upgrade, $2.2 million was paid to four Nigerian companies – Edington Limited, Biosynthesis Nigeria Limited, Remington Limited and FDZ Nigeria Limited–on the Executive Secretary's instruction for jobs earlier done on the upgrade of PTI. The four companies were discovered to have given fictitious addresses, while jobs purportedly completed were never done."[31] So between 2002 and 2005, more than N876.4 million was reportedly expended, with Univation executing only the educational and curriculum upgrades and ignoring the construction aspect while the company was paid in full.[32] In another instance, a contract for the supply of computers was said to have been split into 10 pieces in equal terms, and a printing contract awarded to Garajo Nigeria Limited was executed and paid for without approval, while the auditors found no evidence of supply.[33]

Obasanjo Library Scandal

The multi-billion naira presidential library project launched by Obasanjo while he was still in office fetched the former president another round of criticism by commentators. To Tam David-West, the way the former president raised the sum of over N6 billion leaves much to be desired.[34] Donations by agencies like NNPC and NPA, among others, were questioned in massive corruption scandals and left a huge mark on Obasanjo's administration. David-West even wondered if Obasanjo could reconcile the contradiction that while his government was probing the NPA for an alleged multi-billion naira fraud, the NPA was donating one million pounds in foreign hard currency for his library project.[35]

National ID Card Scam

The national identity card project was viewed as the drainpipe down which public funds disappeared due to Obasanjo's government. Some members of the National Assembly reportedly warned that the project, inherited from the previous military regime, had become a means of stealing public funds. Despite this warning, Obasanjo went ahead with implementation.[36] By the year 2000, when the request for N18 billion went before the

Senate, Obasanjo had already released N6 billion to Internal Affairs for the project. By 2003, it had attained the monumental expenditure level of a scandalous N24 billion.[37] It was reported that a former director in the Department of National Civil Registration, Christopher Agidi, received sums of money in both dollars and naira to influence the award of the ID card contract to Sagem SA of France.[38]

In a rather dramatic twist, Adeniyi Adelagun, the Nigerian business partner of Sagem SA, revealed in his defense before the Senate Committee that "part of the $214 billion bribe money collected in the National ID card scam was used in the persecution of the PDP's 'operation capture southwest' spearheaded by late Afolabi into whose foreign account in the United Kingdom the payment of $345,000 was made."[39]

Fraudulent Road Contracts

Other arteries of corruption during Obasanjo's tenure were contracts awarded for construction of federal roads. It has been noted that the Work and Housing Ministry had a total contractual commitment of about N352 billion for federal roads between 1999 and 2003 at a time Chief Tony Anenih was minister, but the Ministry reportedly claimed that funds paid out for all completed works and ongoing projects was N118.42 billion.[40]

A document submitted by Ibrahim Dankwambo, the accountant general of the federation at the time, has it that the Obasanjo administration spent about N900 billion on roads while they were at the same time indebted to contractors to the tune of N950 billion, a situation described by Thisday Newspaper as "antithetical to be so hugely indebted to road contractors with almost all the roads in the country virtually impassable."[41]

Questionable Privatization Program

Obasanjo's administration chose to privatize some public utilities, resulting in the establishment of the Bureau of Private Enterprises (BPE). As Akpan reports, the program was implemented in such a manner that some public assets were handed over to private owners at ridiculously low prices.[42] It was believed in some quarters that most of the "investors" were business associates of members of Obasanjo's family.[43] The House of Representatives Committee on Communications, which probed the privatization of the Nigerian Telecommunication Commission (NITEL) to the Dutch firm Pentascope, discovered that the company was only three months old when BPE advertised for expression of interests, and that it was registered outside Nigeria on January 1, 2002, a worldwide public holiday. It was also found to have a workforce of only eight persons, including its janitor.[44] Again, Pentascope was not even registered to do business in Nigeria as required by the Companies and Allied Matters Act.[45]

The Aluminum Smelter Company of Nigeria, worth $3.2 billion, was handed over to Russell, a Russian firm, for a paltry $250 million. The company was asked to pay $130 million and then use the balance of $120 million to dredge the Imo River for easy transportation of goods.[46] It has, however, emerged that Russell neither carried out the dredging nor refunded the $120 million.[47]

Finally, there is the case of the Delta Steel Company. The GIHL never bid but mysteriously acquired it, while the federal government's 5% equity in the Eleme Petroleum Chemical Limited (EPCL) was sold to Indorama for $265 million.[48]

NICON Insurance, which was bought in 2006 by billionaire businessman Jimoh Ibrahim for $46.88 million, was another major tradeoff of key national assets in the privatization program. In fact, then Director-General of BPE Bolanle Onagoruwa confessed to a

Senate committee that so far, N2.3 billion was diverted in the NICON sale.[49]

Tafa Balogun Saga

Mustafa Adebayo Balogun, popularly known as Tafa Balogun, became Inspector General of Police (IGP) in March of 2002, replacing Musiliu Smith. On April 4, 2005, Balogun was arraigned in Federal High Court for stealing and laundering over $100 million in his three years as IGP.[50] The EFCC brought 70 charges against him. Balogun took a plea bargain with the court in exchange for returning much of the property and money,[51] and was subsequently sentenced to six months imprisonment.

COJA Fraudulent Contracts

In a petition written against President Obasanjo by the Coalition Against Corrupt Leaders, it was alleged that over N56 billion was squandered on the 8th African Games in Abuja. According to the petition, "when the game was held in Abuja in 2003, most of the disbursements made did not follow due process... Most of the contracts were found to be inflated, at an average of 500 per cent. At the end of the day, more than 56 billion naira could not be accounted for by Obasanjo, his son Gbenja, and Amos Adamu, the Executive Director of COJA."[52]

This could be seen as a way of siphoning public funds through the awarding of contracts without due process. As observed by Tam David-West, COJA, headed by Amos Adamu, then Director of Sports Development, awarded a N200 million contract for mobile toilets to be used at the games; a Lagos-based company also bagged a contract of N104.4 million, while Teju Foam earned N264.8 million just to provide mattresses.[53]

Halliburton Bribe Scandal

The administration of Obasanjo was not spared in the Halliburton bribe scandal, as millions were paid to top Nigerian functionaries by Kellogg Brown, a subsidiary of Halliburton, to facilitate four liquefied Natural Gas contracts at Bonny Island between 1994 and 2004, violating the Foreign Corrupt Practices Act.[54]

Political Office Holders Implicated During Obasanjo Administration

Many political leaders were investigated and linked to corruption during Obasanjo's administration. They include Vice President Atiku Abubakar; Governor of Abia State Orji Uzor Kalu; Governor of Bayelsa State Diepreye Alamieyeseigha; Governor of Plateau State Joshua Dariye; Governor of Ekiti State Ayo Fayose; Governor of Jigawa State Saminu Turaki; Governor of Taraba State Jolly Nyame; Governor of Zamfara State Sani Yerima; Governor of Kogi State Abubakar Audu; Governor of Borno State Modu Sheriff; Governor of Edo State Lucky Igbinedion; and Governor of Delta State James Ibori.[55] Other notable scandals included Senate President Adolphus Wabara and Minister of Education Prof. Fabian Osuji, who were relieved of their responsibilities after being implicated in a bribery scandal.

Umaru Musa Yar'Adua Administration (2007-2010)

Cases of corruption during the administration of Umaru Musa Yar'Adua from May 29, 2007 until his death on May 5, 2010 were mostly the manifestations of the hangover of Obasanjo's administration. One reason is that Yar'Adua's ascension to power was devised by Obasanjo after his bid for a third term failed. The election that produced Yar'Adua was marred by widespread fraud and malpractice. Even Yar'Adua, at his swearing-in ceremony, openly acknowledged that his election was flawed.[56] It was revealed that Supreme Court justices were bribed to legitimize the corrupt elections that led to his presidency.[57]

The corrupt elements that led to Yar'Adua's administration stayed active. Indeed, one of the allegations of corruption against President Yar'adua was his connection with ex-governors who had been deemed corrupt.[58] Cases of corruption were rife under Yar'Adua, who was ailing through much of his administration.

Ribadu's Controversial Sack

It was alleged in some quarters that then-EFCC Chairman Nuhu Ribadu, who was very active in the anti-corruption campaign, was sacked by the president for his refusal to back off from pursuing corruption charges against James Ibori, former governor of Delta State and a close ally of Yar'Adua. Ribadu's termination came on December 27, 2007, just 15 days after Ibori's arrest. The former EFCC boss disclosed before a London court that Ibori tried to bribe him in 2007 with $15 million in cash in a bag so heavy one man alone could not lift it.[59]

As Ribadu was relieved of the EFCC top job and Farida Waziri installed in his stead, aspersion was cast on Yar'Adua's credibility in fighting corruption. According to an unpublished statement attributed to a member of the US State Department and leaked by Olusegun Adeniyi in his book Power, Politics & Death, Washington had reservations about the EFCC and felt the need to review assistance and interactions with the commission. The statement reads:

"The United States Government (USG) is strongly concerned for the independence and integrity of the Economic and Financial Crimes Commission (EFCC) in terms of perception and of the institution's continued credible performance.

The United States is concerned that the momentum behind EFCC's robust investigation and prosecution of high profile cases involving corruption and fraud issues has been curbed significantly this year. Other than one recent arrest, we have not seen any progress on EFCC prosecutions of over a dozen former governors and senior officials, some of whom seem to retain sizable Government of Nigeria's influence.

Consequently, we believe these trends jeopardize not only President Yar'Adua's Seven-point agenda for reform but also lead to questions regarding the credibility of the Government of Nigeria itself. The most recent massive redeployments of EFCC staff have left a shell of inexperienced replacements at best in most areas, wasting considerable United States Government and international training, threatening the EFCC's institutional integrity, jeopardizing cooperation efforts. Additionally, with the EFCC leadership having been completely reassigned, it will take considerable time to build new relationships and trust with the new EFCC leadership. Given the situation, the United States is reviewing all its interactions and assistance with the EFCC. We are therefore extremely reluctant to consider additional requests for resources or training until the EFCC can demonstrate genuine effort or high-profile prosecutions (including prominent ex-governors), extraditions and the establishment of criminal procedures through credible timelines and benchmarks..."[60]

Aondoakaa Factor

Michael Kaase Aondoakaa was appointed attorney general of the federation and the Minister of Justice on July 26, 2007 by President Yar'Adua. He served in the executive council until February 10, 2010, when he was relieved of the job in controversial circumstances by acting President Goodluck Jonathan.

In an article in Streetjournal Magazine, Aondoakaa was deemed to go down in history as the most corrupt attorney general in the history of Nigeria, and was also accused of helping former governors evade prosecution for their money laundering and other corrupt activities.[61]

A civil society group, Global Integrity Crusade Network, in a petition to the EFCC chairman dated August 13, 2019, said available information shows that Aondoakaa interfered in many EFCC prosecutions and destroyed cases relating to corrupt state governors, mostly by discontinuing hearings and trials, even without clear power to do so.[62]

While doubting President Yar'Adua's sincerity in the fight against corruption, the late president's spokesperson, Oluscgun Adcniyi, confessed that the appearance of scheming between Aondoakaa and Ibori was destroying the reputation of the government and compromising his personal integrity.[63]

Peter Odili Corruption Case

Peter Odili was the governor of Rivers State between 1999 and 2007, and he was alleged to have moved about N4 billion in cash to favor his aide-de-camp Isaac Onyesom as well as Emmanuel Nkata, who worked in the Rivers State liaison office in Abuja.[64] The EFCC also alleged that N1.5 billion was used by the former Rivers State governor to obtain a doctorate degree and to get a hall named after him at Lincoln University in the United States.[65]

Wole Arisekola pointed out that it was former Attorney General Aondoakaa that saved Odili from the EFCC in "another ploy to shield his partner in crime."[66] On February 22, 2007, Odili filed a suit challenging the powers of the EFCC to probe his administration. The lawsuit, according to Arisekola, took place quietly and was rarely reported by the media, and the federal court judge overseeing the case fast-tracked it, quickly delivering a 122-page ruling in Odili's favor.[67]

James Ibori Question

Although James Ibori served as governor of Delta State from 1999 to 2007, most of his many sins in office came to light during Yar'Adua's administration. After about five years of playing hide and seek with Nigerian and British authorities, Ibori pled guilty to 10 counts of money laundering and conspiracy to defraud, admitting that he stole about $250 million.[68] As reported by the Premium Times, the Metropolitan Police accused Ibori of using of the stolen money to buy six houses in London, paying £2.2m in cash for one Hampstead mansion, and putting his children in expensive British private schools.[69] The prosecution eventually discontinued Ibori's trial because the former governor "accepted the entirety of the prosecution's case as it has always been set out."[70]

James Ibori served as a political associate of the late President Yar'Adua despite being indicted by the former Chairman of EFCC, Nuhu Ribadu, and it is against this backdrop that Yar'Adua fired Ribadu.[71]

Lucky Igbinedion

In January 2008, former Edo State governor Lucky Igbinedion, who held office between 1999 and 2007, was declared wanted by the EFCC on charges of financial fraud and with stealing up to N4.4 billion.[72] At the ruling, Igbinedion was fined N3.5 million and lost merely three properties.[73] According to SaharaReporters, Igbinedion struck a private deal with EFCC chair Farida Waziri.[74] This was believed to be the reason for the former governor's lenient sentence.

Boni Haruna Fraud Allegation

In August 2008, the EFCC accused Boni Haruna of stealing N93 million between 1999 and 2007 when he served as governor of Adamawa State, the home state of former vice president Atiku Abubakar.[75] Haruna was reportedly a close ally to Abubakar, and was the ninth governor who served during the term of President Obasanjo to face graft charges.[76]

Alamieyeseigha Drama

In July 2007, former Bayelsa governor Diepreye Alamieyeseigha, who served from 1999 until his impeachment in 2005, pled guilty to corruption charges filed against him. He was sentenced to two years in jail, all of it time already served. [77] In September 2005, the UK's metropolitan police detained Alamieyeseigha after finding about £1 million cash on him, and another £1.8 million elsewhere in cash and accounts.[78] He was subsequently charged with money laundering but he jumped bail, reportedly disguising himself in woman's clothing and returning to Nigeria.

Patricia Etteh Saga

Following an investigation in October of 2009 by a nine-member probe panel, Patricia Olubunmi Etteh, the first ever female speaker of the House of Representatives, was found to have violated House rules by awarding contracts worth $5 million for renovation of her official residence and the purchase of at least ten cars.[79] Consequently, Etteh and her deputy, Babangida Nguroje, hurriedly resigned to avoid being impeached. As she left the chamber, she was greeted with jeers and boos by a horde of National Assembly staff that clustered in the lobby.[80]

Re-Looting Of Tafa Balogun's Loot

The Tafa Balogun saga took another twist when in February of 2009, Chairman of the House Committee on Police Affairs Abdul Ahmed Ningi asked Inspector General of Police Mike Okiro to provide details of the money recovered from Balogun, a request that he passed to EFCC chair Farida Waziri.[81] The EFCC stated, however, that they did not have records of the exact properties recovered from Balogun.[82] It was alleged that some of the houses had been secretly sold at give-away prices, so in April of 2009, a House committee invited Balogun, Okiro and Waziri to explain how the N16 billion allegedly recovered from Balogun went missing.[83]

Corruption In Aviation Ministry

Former aviation minister Babalola Borishade; former managing director of NAMA T.A. Dairo; assistant to Borishade Ronald Iyayi; and George Eider were arraigned in 2008 for indulging in bribery, forgery, and other activities designed to enrich themselves.[84] They were said to have benefited from the N6.5 billion safe tower project. Borishade was first arrested and arraigned in June of 2008 alongside Chief Femi Fani-Kayode, who succeeded Borishade in the Ministry of Aviation. This happened shortly after the Senate committee was probing issues with the N19.5 billion Aviation Intervention Fund in Abuja.[85]

Health Ministry N300 Million Scandal

In February of 2008, the EFCC was ordered to probe then-Minister of Health Adenike Grange and Minister of State Gabriel Aduku for corruption. By March of 2008, the two ministers tendered their resignations following media reports that that the EFCC had questioned Grange and other top health officials for allegedly spending N300 million of the ministry's 2007 budget on dubious contracts and Christmas gifts contrary to presidential directive.[86]

According to Reuters, Nigerian newspapers also named more than a dozen federal legislators, including Iyabo Obasanjo, former President Olusegun Obasanjo's daughter and chair of the Senate committee on health, as beneficiaries of the illegal spending spree.[87]

Goodluck Jonathan's Administration (2010-2015)

Media reports attributed to the United Kingdom's Department for International Development has estimated a total of about $32 billion to have been lost to corruption during the six-year administration of President Goodluck Jonathan.[88] Years after leaving office, condemnation continues to trail Jonathan and his government over mindless looting and fiscal impropriety. His administration has often been criticized, especially by members of the ruling All Progressives Congress (APC), as the most corrupt in the history of Nigeria. Numerous scandals were recorded during Jonathan's administration, which culminated in its discontinuation in 2015. Corruption was rampant in the oil sector, including mismanagement of security funds and funds that went missing altogether.

Petroleum Subsidy Scam

Ngozi Okonjo-Iweala, who served as Finance Minister under Goodluck Jonathan's administration, revealed that Nigeria's 2011 oil subsidies came to a frightening total of N1.73 trillion, of which kerosene subsidies were N310.4 billion, representing 2.7% of the federal government's budget.[89] In January of 2012, President Jonathan announced a subsidy phase-out, which sparked nationwide protest. One of the most controversial issues was alleged fraud in the oil subsidy program, which went beyond the smuggling of oil into neighboring countries such as Benin and

Niger, where prices were much higher.[90] Allegations were rife that companies were claiming subsidies for shipments of oil and kerosene never delivered, and allegations swirled that corrupt payments were made to control the rights to import subsidized kerosene to companies who then sold it to consumers at non-subsidized prices.[91]

Suspecting this, the House of Representatives set up the Ad-Hoc Committee to Verify and Determine the Actual Subsidy Requirements under Resolution No.HR.1/2012. The committee, chaired by Farouk Lawan from Kano State, found that the subsidy regime was fraught with endemic corruption and entrenched inefficiency, deeming that N1.067 trillion was misappropriated during the period under review.[92]

Lawan Farouk Bribery Scandal

Lawan Farouk, the chairman of the committee noted above, was famed for his zero-tolerance approach to corruption. In fact, Lawan also chaired a self-styled "Integrity Group" within the House, a group dedicated to transparency and good governance.[93]

Ironically, a scandal broke out with Farouk at the center following the investigation of the oil subsidy scam. As recounted by Okonjo-Iweala, Nigerian businessmen Femi Otedola accused Lawan of demanding a bribe of $3 million to facilitate the committee's removal of the names of his two companies, Zeno Oil and Gas Ltd and Synopsis Enterprises Ltd, from the list of companies to be sanctioned.[94] Lawan initially denied the charge, but when a video was leaked showing him and an associate purportedly receiving $620,000 of the $3 million bribe from Otedola, Lawan said he took this money to show the EFCC and other authorities the type of pressure the committee was put under to stop the investigation or remove company names from the list of offenders. The House of Representatives, however, found this explanation less than credible since records showed that at an earlier House session, Lawan had asked for two company names to be expunged from the Committee's report.[95]

Missing $20 Billion Saga

One of the many incidents of corruption that badly stained Goodluck Jonathan's government was the $20 billion reportedly missing from the NNPC accounts. This saga of the missing oil revenue was blown open by Mallam Lamido Sanusi, governor of the Central Bank of Nigeria at the time. Initially, Sanusi alerted the President on September 25, 2013 that there was $49.8 billion missing from the country's oil accounts for the period from January 2012 to July 2013.[96] When a technical task force was set up at the insistence of the finance minister, they looked at all the evidence for sums that were unaccounted for among the funds that the NNPC should have disbursed, then tried to reconcile all numbers from the three agencies.[97] The task force reported in a week, and in the press conference that followed, Lamido Sanusi admitted that his staff had made a mistake. After the reconciliation, the CBN had to accept that the unaccounted-for funds that were due to the federation were about $12 billion.[98]

While appearing before a Senate committee on February 4, 2014, however, Sanusi said although the unaccounted-for funds were not $12 billion but about $20 billion.[99] This led to President Jonathan suspending Sanusi for financial recklessness and misconduct. PricewaterhouseCoopers was engaged to carry out the forensic investigation into the missing $20 billion on behalf of the federal government. In February 2015, Solomon Olamilekan, chairman of the House Committee on Public Accounts, told reporters that the Office of the Auditor-General of the Federation only presented a "highly-condensed version" of the report to the public, recalling that in the condensed version, the NNPC was directed to remit a "minimum of $1.4 billion into the Federation Account."[100]

Malabu Oil Scam

In this major scandal, President Goodluck Jonathan was directly accused of collecting bribes along with other key government figures including former attorney general Mohammed Bello Adoke and former petroleum minister Diezani Alison-Madueke. How did this bribery scandal start? It started when former petroleum minister Dan Etete, appointed by dictator Sani Abacha, acquired an oil block through his company Malabu Oil and Gas Limited while in office in 1998. The deal was reportedly struck only five days after the company was incorporated with three shareholders: Mohammed Sani Abacha, Kweku Amafagha (a fake name created by Etete) and Hassan Hindu, wife of a former Nigerian High Commissioner to the UK.[101] The oil block, which was said to contain about nine billion barrels of crude oil, was sold to Shell and ENI for $1.3 billion in 2011. The two companies paid the money to an account belonging to the federal government of Nigeria at JP Morgan in London.[102] At the same time, the government under Goodluck Jonathan transferred $801 million into accounts controlled by Malabu and Etete in Nigeria. Proceeds from this scam were allegedly shared with various public officials in Nigeria as bribes. Goodluck Jonathan was accused of receiving up to $200 million from the controversial deal.[103]

SURE-P Funds Mismanagement

On the heels of the January 2012 protests over subsidy removal on petroleum products, the President called for negotiation sessions with the Nigerian Labor Union at which the groups reached a compromise whereby the government pulled back from a total phase-out to a 50% phase-out of the subsidies on refined petroleum.[104] The government agreed that the money saved would be applied to expenditures in transportation, maternal and child health, and employment creation, and be used to boost infrastructure and other investments that would benefit the society at large.[105] It was decided that the management of the program be separated from the budget and that a committee comprising of labor, civil society, and a cross-section of Nigerians be set up to oversee and manage the funds. This program came to be known as the Subsidy Reinvestment and Empowerment Program, popularly known as SURE-P.

Unfortunately, there came a time when the ICPC had to probe the activities of some senior officials of SURE-P. The probe was in connection with N3 billion worth of fraud, allegedly involving the Federal Ministry of Finance and the SURE-P Graduate Internship Scheme funds, which was meant to pay an allowance to 17,500 participants for the term of eight months.[106]

Diezani Alison-Madueke and Allegations of Corruption

Diezani Alison-Madueke served as petroleum minister under Goodluck Jonathan's administration and appeared to be the face of corruption at the time. She has been linked to scandalous financial crimes while in office. According to a report by PBS NewsHour, she may have personally supervised the looting of $6 billion from Nigeria's coffers.[107] It was under Alison-Madueke's supervision that about $20 billion reportedly went missing in the oil sector through an NNPC account, an event that led to the sacking of CBN governor Lamido Sanusi.

In the build-up to the 2015 presidential election, Alison-Madueke was alleged to have stashed away about $115 million, with instructions to distribute the money among electoral officials in the 36 states of the federation to rig the election in favor of Goodluck Jonathan, though Jonathan, the incumbent, wound up losing to Muhammadu Buhari.[108]

In 2017, a Lagos court ordered the final forfeiture of a $37.5 million apartment complex on Banana Island allegedly purchased by Alison-Madueke between 2011 and 2012 while she was still in office.[109] The court ordered that rent proceeds from the apartment building totaling nearly $3 million be forfeited as well.[110]

In July 2017, Alison-Madueke was named in a US Department of Justice lawsuit seeking to reclaim assets worth $144 million believed to have been proceeds of corrupt dealings, with assets including a $50 million luxury condo in New York and an $80 million yacht purchased by Nigerian businessmen believed to have received lucrative oil contracts from Nigeria's state oil company largely thanks to Alison-Madueke's influence.[111]

Dasukigate

Dasukigate involves the mismanagement and embezzlement of $2.1 billion placed under the care of the former National Security Adviser Sambo Dasuki. In this scandal, an illegal arms procurement deal was brought to light by the interim report of the Presidential Investigations Committee on Arms Procurement under the Goodluck Jonathan administration. This committee, set up by President Buhari in 2015, revealed that extra-budgetary spending to the tune of N643.8 billion - including additional spending of about $2.1 billion, supposedly meant for the procurement of arms to fight the Boko Haram insurgency - was squandered. President Buhari ordered the arrest of Sambo Dasuki and he was apprehended in December 2015. Below are the names of those linked to the arms deal:

- Attahiru Bafarawa, former governor of Sokoto State, arrested December 1, 2015. Continues to stand trial alongside Dasuki.
- High Chief Raymond Dokpesi, charged December 10, 2015 on six counts related to receiving N2.1 billion to run PDP media campaign.
- Iyiola Omisore, former deputy governor of Osun State,

arrested on July 4, 2016 over receiving N700 million in stolen funds from the Office of the NSA. He claims to have returned N300 million, and charges against him have subsequently been dropped.

- Former Chief of Air Staff Adesola Amosu, arrested late January 2016. $1 million found in his apartment.
- Lara Amosu, his wife, arrested early in February 2016. N3 billion found in bank accounts held in trust for her husband.
- Air Vice Marshal J.B. Adigun, Chief of Account and Budget of the Nigerian Air Force, arrested late January 2016.
- Air Commodore O. Gbadebo, in the custody of EFCC while standing trial alongside Amosu.
- Chief Olisa Metuh, spokesperson for the PDP, tried for receiving N400 million under Armsgate. Convicted of money laundering and criminal diversion of funds, sentenced to seven years imprisonment.
- Major General Yishau Mahmood Abubakar, property seized by the EFCC in January 2016. Died in car crash in March 2016.
- Colonel Ojogbane Adegbe, a former aide-de-camp to President Goodluck Jonathan, arrested February 2016 by the EFCC. Released shortly afterward and never charged. Adegbe later counter-sued the EFCC, claiming political motivation in his arrest.
- Haliru Bello, former chairman of the PDP, on trial since April 2016 for receiving N300 million into accounts of his companies.
- Waripamowei Dudafa, former special advisor to Goodluck Jonathan, convicted of sharing in N10 billion taken from the office of the NSA and given to PDP candidates.
- Bala James Ngillari, former governor of Adamawa State, charged by EFCC for receiving N450 million from Armsgate. Acquitted on appeal.

·   Aminu Babakusa, former executive director at the Nigerian National Petroleum Corporation, allegedly received N2.2 billion which he claimed he "shared out as instructed." Continues to stand trial alongside Dasuki. An updated charge-sheet alleges responsibility for N33.2 billion in misappropriated funds.[112]

Other politicians and statesmen involved in the saga, named by PMnews Nigeria, are:

·   Ex-Oyo State governor Rasheed Ladoja, allegedly received N100m
·   Ex-Rivers governor Peter Odili (N100m)
·   Ex-Zamfara governor Mahmud Aliyu Shinkafi (N100m)
·   Ex-Anambra governor Jim Nwobodo (N500m)
·   Chief Tony Anenih (N260m)
·   Ex-PDP BoT chairman Chief Tony Anenih (N260m)
·   Ex-PDP National Chairman Ahmadu Ali (N100m)
·   Chief Bode George (N100m)
·   Yerima Abdullahi (N100m)
·   Chief Olu Falae (N100m)
·   Tanko Yakasai (N63m)
·   General Bello Sarkin Yaki (N200m)
·   Iyorchia Ayu's company (N345m)
·   BAM Properties (N300m)
·   Dalhatu Investment Limited (N1.5b)
·   Sagir Attahiru (N300m)
·   Former Chairman of the House of Representatives on Security and Intelligence Bello Matawalle (N300m)
·   ACACIA Holdings (N600m)
·   Bashir Yuguda (N1,950,000)[113]

This list is partial, and could be inexhaustible. The EFCC also accused Dasuki of awarding phantom contracts to buy 12 helicopters, four fighter jets, and ammunition, but he denied those allegations.[114]

Maina Pension Scam

Abdulrasheed Maina was chairman of the Pension Reform Task Force Team constituted in 2010 to investigate pension accounts at the Office of the Head of Civil Service of the Federation and that of the police. Maina was accused by the EFCC of stealing about N14 billion from pension accounts through several illegal payments to fake pensioners, non-existing contracts, and other pension reform unions, while diverting some of the stolen funds through 66 bank accounts with the aid of the former head of service Stephen Oronsaye. This startling revelation was made by prosecution witness Rouqayyah Ibrahim, an investigator with the EFCC.[115]

Maina was under prosecution alongside his firm, Common Input Property and Investment Ltd, on a 12-count charge of operating fictitious bank accounts, corruption, and money laundering to the tune of N2 billion.[116]

Another EFCC operative, Mohammed Goji, revealed in December of 2019 how Abdulrasheed Maina illegally acquired several properties in the name of his son, Faisal.[117]

In his testimony, Goji said, "During the investigation of Abdulrasheed Maina, who was involved in a complex web of money laundering, which include movement of funds from the police pension account as well as the accounts of the pension office of the Office of the Head of Service of the Federation to corporate entities as payment for biometric enrollment; payment of collective allowances and payment of contracts, which were fraudulent."[118]

Maina was on the run during his trial but he was arrested in Niger on November 30, 2020 through a collaborative effort of the operatives of the Nigeria Police Force, INTERPOL NCB, Abuja, and their counterpart in Niger. His arrest followed a court order that declared him wanted over failure to appear for his hearing after he was granted bail.[119]

Police Pension Fund Scandal

A series of probes by the National Assembly culminating in 2013 revealed a serious level of corruption in the Defined Benefits Pension Scheme, finding that at least N32 billion had been fraudulently diverted then stolen by unscrupulous civil servants and their collaborators.[120] Earlier in March 2012, about five people were arraigned on charges of "conspiracy and criminal breach of trust for the roles they played in pension fraud."[121] They include John Yakubu Yusuf, a former assistant director in the federal civil service who was tried on a 20-count charge alongside Atiku Abubakar Kigo (permanent secretary), Ahmed Inuwa Wada (director), Veronica Onyegbula (cashier) and Sani Habila Zira (ICT officer).[122] Yusuf's sentencing came after he pleaded guilty to betraying trust and fraudulently converting N2 billion of police pension funds to private use, and the trial continued for the other accused.[123] He was initially convicted and sentenced to two years imprisonment with a fine of N750,000 in a plea-bargain arrangement.[124] He was also asked to forfeit property valued at N325 million, including 32 houses.[125] The conviction, considered to be a slap on the wrist, sparked national and international outrage.[126]

The Stella Oduah Debacle

Stella Oduah was appointed by Goodluck Jonathan, deploying to the Ministry of Aviation on July 4, 2011. She was fired on February 12, 2014 after the Nigeria Civil Aviation Authority procured BMW armoured cars for her at inflated prices.[127] Oduah was indicted along with the Nigerian subsidiary of Chinese construction giant CCECC in alleged fraudulent cash transactions of about N5 billion over five months in 2014.[128] Oduah, who was elected to the Senate in 2015 even as the scandal raged, has always maintained her innocence. She said in response to a query in 2013 that the procurement was duly provided for in the budget of that year.[129]

N676m NIS Recruitment Scam

The March 2014 recruitment exercise of Nigeria Immigration Service (NIS) was considered a national disaster after thousands of applicants seeking employment stampeded the recruitment centers, where at least 16 were killed. Beyond the tragedy, Interior Minister Abba Moro allegedly collected N676.6 million from 676,675 job seekers in the ill-fated exercise. Each of the applicants that participated in the fatal NIS recruitment exercise was required to pay N1,000 to obtain an online registration form.

Following a short detention in February of 2016, Moro was arraigned before the Federal High Court, where the EFCC slammed an 11-count charge on him and four others.

Moro faced trial alongside Anastasia Daniel-Nwobia, a former permanent secretary in the ministry; F.O. Alayebami, a deputy director in the ministry; Mahmood Ahmadu, who had been at large; and Drexel Tech Nigeria Limited, a firm involved in the disaster. Charges included money laundering, abuse of office, procurement fraud and fraud against Nigerian applicants to the tune of N675,000.[130]

During the trial, Moro confessed that the recruitment exercise of Nigeria Immigration Service was marred by controversies, nepotism, job racketeering, and lopsidedness.[131] In his words, "The controversies had derailed recruitment exercise even before I became the Minister of Interior."[132]

Bad Arms Deal In South Africa

Another incident that reflected poorly on Jonathan's government was when $9.3 million in cash was allegedly smuggled into South Africa using a private jet belonging to Pastor Ayo Oritsejafor, former president of the Christian Association of Nigeria. The money was meant for the purchase of arms for the Nigerian Intelligence Services to fight Boko Haram, but the aircraft that conveyed it was not declared in South Africa until immigration officials discovered it.[133] The cash, distributed in $100 bills stashed in suitcases, was seized at Lanseria Airport north of Johannesburg.[134] In the following month, the Asset Forfeiture Unit of the National Prosecuting Authority seized $5.7 million for yet another arms deal between South Africa and Nigeria.[135] The South African High Commissioner in Nigeria, Lulu Mnguni, who appeared on an African Independent Television (AIT) news program following the incident, said his country had no intention of keeping the seized funds but would only release them to Nigeria after due process had been followed.[136]

Although the money was claimed to have been meant for arms dealing between Nigeria and South Africa, the government of South Africa has denied its involvement in any deal with the Nigerian government, while all efforts to investigate the fraud at the legislative chamber were frustrated by the political party in power.[137]

Muhammadu Buhari Administration (From 2015)

By the time Muhammadu Buhari took office, Nigerians were weary of endemic corruption. Scandals relentlessly pervaded democratic dispensations, and life was tough for common Nigerians. Corruption during Goodluck Jonathan's administration appeared to reach apogee, and there was a conscious need to halt the trend. Then came Muhammadu Buhari, a no-nonsense old soldier who was believed to have the capability and clout to tackle corruption head-on. Buhari's campaign promise in 2015 hinged majorly on the fight against corruption, and it was generally believed that if he emerged as president, there would be rapid crackdown on corrupt elements in the country. Unfortunately, corruption remains. Though early efforts in the fight against corruption showed promise, the tempo died down more quickly than expected. Corruption soon assumed comical and embarrassing dimensions. The administration that postured against corruption soon embroiled itself in massive scandals.

N36 Million 'Swallowed' By Snake

After all the promises to fight corruption, it was a big blow to Buhari's government when it was reported in February 2018 that a mysterious intruder sneaked into the accounts office of the Joint Admissions and Matriculation Board in Makurdi, the Benue State capital, and made away with N36 million cash.[138]
As reported by the Daily Post, "a team of auditors was dispatched to different state offices of JAMB to take inventory of the sold and unsold scratch cards and recover whatever money that might have either been generated or mismanaged during the period of the sale of scratch cards.

> *"On their visit to Makurdi office of JAMB, a sales clerk, Philomina Chieshe, told JAMB registrar and his team that she could not account for N36 million she made in previous years before the abolition of scratch cards.*
> *"Philomina in her confessional statement said that Joan Asen and her accomplices confessed that they have been stealing the money 'spiritually' through a mysterious snake that always sneak into the office to swallow the money from the vault."[139]*

In the previous year, it was said that a rat infestation of the Aso Villa forced the President to work from home. This would mark the era in which animals contributed their quota to those blamed for corruption in Nigeria.

Monkeys 'Swallowed' N70 Million, Too

After the shocking and false confession that Asen used a mysterious snake to swallow N36 million from the Board's vault, another N70 million was gathered by northern senators from the 7th Senate and handed over to northern senators of the 8th Senate. Senator Shehu Sani from Kaduna State told reporters that monkeys swallowed the money at the senator's farm.[140]

Even A Gorilla 'Swallowed' N6.8 Million

A gorilla in a public zoo became the center of yet another corruption crisis in Nigeria after officials of Kano Zoological Garden said the primate swallowed about N6.8 million worth of gate fees collected from patrons of the zoo, especially during Eid-al-Fitr festivities in June of 2019.

Following confirmation that the money was missing, state governor Abdullahi Ganduje reportedly ordered the anti-corruption commission to open a probe into the issue.[141]

N544 Million Grass-Cutting Scam

In 2017, the country was stunned when a senate ad-hoc committee alleged that Secretary to the Government of the Federation (SGF) Babachir Lawal awarded contracts worth over N544 million to companies in which he had interest. The contract, according to the senate committee, was to "remove invasive plant species" from the Yobe State water channels.[142] Following the allegation, the presidency set up a three-man committee to investigate the matter.

The committee was chaired by Vice President Yemi Osinbajo with the reigning attorney general and Minister of Justice serving as well.

After the president accepted the recommendation of the panel, he terminated Lawal's appointment on October 20, 2017, appointing Boss Mustapha in his place. The EFCC further prosecuted Lawal for fraudulently converting cumulative proceeds of grass-cutting contracts worth about N544 million, which he allegedly also awarded to companies in which he had interest. The anti-graft agency slammed a 10-count charge on Lawal with allegations of fraud, diversion of over N544 million, and criminal conspiracy.

Others standing trial were his younger brother, Hamidu Lawal, as well as Suleiman Abubakar, Apch Monday, and two companies: Rholavision Engineering Ltd and Josmon Technologies Ltd. [143] They were initially arraigned before FCT High Court in Abuja on February 13, 2019.

Ikoyigate

Ayodele Oke, head of the National Intelligence Agency, was suspended on April 19, 2017 after the EFCC found about $43.45 million in a house in Ikoyi, Lagos. The commission later said the house where the money was found was rented in the name of Oke's wife, Folashade, and they eventually secured a court order to ensure the money was forfeited to the federal government.[144]

A panel led by Vice President Osinbajo, however, recommended Oke's dismissal after looking into the circumstances surrounding the cash haul.[145] The panel submitted its report on August 23, 2017, but the President did not act on it until October, when Oke was finally sacked along with Babachir Lawal.

Budget Padding

After the executive arm of government presented the 2016 appropriation bills to legislators, allegations arose that the legislators inflated the proposed budget to accommodate their own interests. The principal officers of the National Assembly were accused of padding and stealing about N481 billion from the 2016 budget.[146] Following a mandamus filed by the Socio-Economic Rights and Accountability Project, the Federal High Court in Lagos ordered President Buhari to probe the indicted lawmakers.

The suit was filed in 2017 after the rights group received information from multiple sources that the Department of State Services and the EFCC had completed investigations into the allegations of padding. They indicted some principal officers of the House of Representatives and the Senate.[147]

'Gandollar' Video Saga

In 2018 Abdullahi Ganduje, the governor of Kano State, became enmeshed in a bribery scandal following a video published by Daily Nigerian showing him taking kickback dollars from a contractor.[148] In the months leading up to the 2019 general elections, social media was abuzz with the video, which was styled 'Gandollar' and sourced by Jaafar Jaafar, a Kano-based journalist and publisher. The video was used mainly by the opposition parties to ridicule the governor, questioning the credibility of the APC-led government in their fight against corruption.

President Buhari and anti-graft agencies were largely silent on the video, but when he finally spoke, he cast doubt on its authenticity and neglected to order an investigation.[149] At the time, the Kano State House of Assembly appeared to be the only institution that pushed for investigation. Rather than allow an investigation however, Ganduje frustrated the assembly by securing a court injunction to stop the probe.[150] He filed a N3 billion defamation suit against Daily Nigerian and its publisher Jaafar over the videos, but suffered defeat when the Kano High Court ordered him to pay N800,000 for expenses incurred by Jaafar and his company, Penlight Media Limited.[151]

Off-the-Mic Episode

The Niger Delta Development Commission, established in the year 2000 to cater to the needs of the indigenous people of the oil-bearing region of the Niger Delta, has remained a cesspool of corruption since inception. Looting, mismanagement of funds, and the approval of expenditures that bring no improvement to the lives of the people of the region are standard practices at the NDDC. Under Buhari's government, the NDDC is still mired in scandal, with managers of the commission indulging in an outrageous squandering of resources meant for the development of the region. An Interim Management Committee (IMC) appointed by President Buhari to midwife the forensic audit of the commission was indicted by the Senate for corruption, financial recklessness, and mismanagement after an open investigation. In it, Nigerians were treated to an egregious display of financial impropriety by the directors of the IMC, led by Professor Kemebradikumo Pondei and Dr. Cairo Ojougboh.[152]

Pondei, before he slumped during grilling at a Senate hearing, confessed that the IMC disbursed the sum of N1.3 billion to staff members, including himself, as bonuses for the Covid-19 pandemic. Further investigations conducted by the Senate and the House of Representatives revealed fraudulent and questionable payments of N81.5 billion by the IMC as well.[153] At the conclusion of its investigation in July of 2020, the Senate resolved that IMC members must refund the N4.923 billion that was criminally spent and then be prosecuted for fraud.[154]

The National Assembly, however, appears to be part of the problem. Senator Godswill Akpabio has even linked members of the National Assembly to brazen corruption and financial irregularities at the NDDC. In his attempt to expose them, Akpabio told lawmakers publicly and to their faces that they are the biggest beneficiaries of the corruption that has rocked the commission.

> *"Who are even the greatest beneficiaries (of these contracts)?" he asked. "It's you people… I just told you that we have records to show that most of the contracts in the NDDC are given out to members of the national assembly…"*

At that point, Thomas Ereyitomi, who represents Warri Federal Constituency, was quick to intercept the minister. Ereyitomi would not allow Mr. Akpabio to open that can of worms. "Honourable Minister, it's okay," he stated, "That is okay…it's okay…Honourable Minister off (sic) your mic."[155]

Maina Reinstatement Saga

The controversial Abdulrasheed Maina, chairman of the Pension Reform Task Force Team, was fired from the Federal Civil Service for abandoning his post and evading arrest following allegations that he embezzled over N2 billion in pension funds during the Goodluck Jonathan administration. Maina fled Nigeria in 2015 and an Interpol warrant was reportedly issued for his arrest, though he still managed to return, enjoying privileges from Buhari's government. Despite the fact that Maina was under investigation for looting pensions during Jonathan's era, he was reinstated and given a double promotion by the Buhari administration until the President terminated his appointment following public outcry, which also prompted the President to order investigation into Maina's reinstatement.

Abba Kyari and the MTN Bribe

Alhaji Abba Kyari, former chief of staff to President Buhari, was investigated by the Special Investigation Panel of the Nigerian police force over an alleged N500 million in bribery money. The bribes were said to have been paid by officials of South African-owned MTN Telecommunications Company, who hoped Kyari would influence the government to discontinue its heavy stance on their $5 billion fine.[156] This was after the Nigerian Communication Commission (NCC) mandated in 2011 that all telecoms operators in Nigeria register all existing phone subscribers before a January 2012 deadline. The sanctions were ordered on MTN due to the company's refusal to comply with a directive to disconnect 5.1 million improperly registered lines before the deadline.[157] The NCC slammed a $5 billion fine on MTN[158] for its failure to comply. The telecommunications giant's bid to fight the huge fine was frustrated, first through the courts and later through diplomatic means. In 2016, Sahara Reporters published the claim that officials of MTN bribed Kyari N500 million to use his relationship with President Buhari to influence the federal government to give MTN a safe landing.[159]

According to the Daily Post, however, Kyari replied that he was helping the All Progressives Congress (APC) raise funds for the gubernatorial election in Bayelsa State, claiming that Buhari was aware of his involvement and did not relieve him of his post.[160]

Onnoghen Scandal

The Anti-Corruption and Research Based Data Initiative, a non-governmental organization, petitioned the government in 2019 about Chief Justice of Nigeria Walter Onnoghen. The group said "We are distressed that facts on the ground indicate the leader of our country's judicial branch is embroiled in suspected financial crimes and breaches of the Code of Conduct Bureau and Tribunal Act.

"The particulars of our findings indicate that: His Lordship Justice Walter Onnoghen is the owner of sundry accounts primarily funded through cash deposits made by himself, up to as recently as 10th August 2016 which appear to have been run in a manner inconsistent with financial transparency and the code of conduct for public officials."[161]

On January 10, 2019, the Nigerian government filed charges against Onnoghen, accusing him of asset declaration offences while pointing out that it was only after the controversial crackdown on judges in 2016 that Onnoghen partially declared his assets. He also failed to declare a series of bank accounts denominated in local and foreign currencies.[162]

Onnoghen allegedly failed to declare his assets in 2009 and 2014 as well.[163]

Meanwhile, Section 15 of the Code of Conduct Bureau and Tribunal Act requires that every public official declare assets on assumption of office and thereafter at the end of every four years.[164] The offence is punishable under Section 23. Danladi Umar, chairman of the Code of Conduct Tribunal (CCT), ordered Onnoghen to forfeit N26.8 million, $137,700, and 13,730 pounds sterling found in his domiciliary account to the federal government. The tribunal, in a unanimous judgment, explained that it ordered forfeiture of the various currencies for Onnoghen's failure to disclose the source of the money throughout the trial. The judgment held that the admission by Onnoghen that he forgot to declare the bank accounts on form CCB001 was a clear contravention of Section 23 of the CCB and CCT Act.[165]

Corruption under a COVID-19 Veil

COVID-19 Fund: Fiscal Support, Palliative Analysis & Institutional Response, a research report produced by BudgIT, a leading advocate for transparency and accountability in Nigeria, laid out concerns that Covid-19 funds in Nigeria were largely mismanaged.

In Premium Times, BudgIT said that as of April 7, 2020, CACOVID, a private coalition of donors and corporate founders, received donations totaling N21.5 billion.[166] They also noted N288 billion in federal disbursements from the N500 billion set aside for the COVID-19 intervention program through its Economic Sustainability Plan, expressing worry over the poor accountability mechanism in the management of the fund: "as of the time of our report, comprehensive details of disbursed funds have not been published on the Open Treasury platform. This further establishes our concerns about the lack of a proper framework for COVID19 fund accountability in Nigeria." [167]

The government claimed it had disbursed N100 billion to beneficiaries of its conditional cash transfer in one week.[168] In a live broadcast by President Buhari in April 2020 amidst nationwide lockdown, he directed an increase in the number of households in the national social register from 2.6 million to 3.6 million. This aroused huge suspicion. Maryam Uwais, the president's special adviser on the social investment program, revealed that just over 700,000 registrants in 2019 could make the number hit 2.6 million.

During the lockdown, life was tough for Nigerians. They were aware that over N31 billion of taxpayers' money had already been expended, and that the majority received nothing. Members of the Nigerian Governors Forum allegedly hoarded those relief materials, throwing the people into starvation. The people, however, did use the EndSARS protest as an opportunity to break into warehouses and loot hoarded food materials in order to satiate their hunger. The mass raids were recorded in Lagos, Abuja, Kogi, Kwara, Osun, Plateau, and Taraba, among others. In Akwa Ibom State, the government held fast to the relief materials, reportedly distributing them to their relatives and cronies as Christmas gifts in December 2020.

Magu In Re-Looting Saga

In a story reminiscent of The Marvelettes's 1967 song the Hunter Gets Captured by the Game, former acting-chairman of the EFCC Ibrahim Magu was destroyed by the very vice against which he fought. Suspicion against him began when the report of the Presidential Committee on Audit of Recovered Assets revealed how interests on N550 billion recovered by the EFCC from May 29, 2015 to November 22, 2018 were allegedly re-looted. The Premium Times states that "Failure to report on the interest on actual lodgments clearly establishes that the interest element of over N550 billion has been re-looted relating to the period under review.

"This is an apparent case of manipulation of data in a very brazen and unprofessional manner and this has greatly eroded the public confidence in the anti-corruption efforts."[169]
Magu was arrested on July 7, 2020 and interrogated by a panel headed by retired justice Ayo Salami on allegations of mismanagement and lack of transparency in managing recovered assets by the commission.[170] He was later suspended and detained.

Buhari's Son-in-Law in $65 Million Saga

Gimba Yau Kumo, who in 2016 married Buhari's daughter Fatima, was the managing director of Federal Mortgage Bank. The Independent Corruption Prosecution Commission (ICPC) said in a statement in May 2021 that Gimba Yau Kumo, Tarry Rufus, and Bola Ogunsola were suspected of misappropriating funds earmarked for a national property development project.[171]

The ICPC statement reads "the persons whose photographs appear above, Tarry Rufus, Mr. Gimba Yau Kumo and Mr. Bola Ogunsola, are hereby declared wanted... in connection with issues relating to the diversion of public funds for real estate to the tune of $65 million."[172]

Hadiza Bala Usman At Centre Of Fraud

President Buhari removed Hadiza Bala Usman as managing director of the Nigerian Ports Authority on May 6, 2021 without stating a reason, but according to Sahara Reporters, at the heart of Usman's suspension appears to be a Cargo Tracking Note (CTN) contract given to a Lebanese syndicate by top government officials.[173]

The online news medium further alleged that the controversial CTN contract was prepared for the Lebanese proxies by Senate President Ahmad Lawan, Minister of Transportation Rotimi Amaechi, and the Minister of Justice and Attorney-General of the Federation Abubakar Malami to rake money into their coffers, adding that "the top government officials had also gotten President Muhammadu Buhari to buy into their deal, which is under the NPA jurisdiction, to swindle the country and its ailing economy."[174]

Sahara Reporters quoted an unnamed source as well: "The Lebanese man will be giving them $300,000 monthly. That was one of the reasons behind Usman's removal. It was a contract on container tracking. But there is still rivalry in the whole contract; there is the Amaechi camp on one side as well as Malami and Senate President on the other side."[175]

Between 2016 and 2017, over N18 billion worth of expenditures at the Nigerian Ports Authority (NPA) was reportedly unexplained under Usman's watch. Consequently, the NPA was investigated for "Excessive Increase in Administrative Expenditure and Operational Expenses."[176]

Usman was first appointed as the NPA boss in 2016, and her tenure was renewed for another five years in January 2021. Following the allegations of corruption, she was suspended and replaced by Mohammed Koko.

The government of Muhammadu Buhari is still running at the time of this writing, so the possibility remains that his profile of corruption will expand by the time he leaves office in 2023.

The compendium of corruption provided in this work is just the tip of the iceberg. It has, however, indicated the depth of corruption in Nigeria, and it has shown the pattern and style with which corruption operates in the country.

CHAPTER FIVE

The Legislature, Another Arm of Corruption

The legislature is another playground for corruption in Nigeria. This arm of government, popular for its purported purpose of providing checks and balances to the system, does not live up to that mission. Many Nigerian legislators find license to steal through the management of zonal intervention projects (ZIPs), otherwise called constituency projects. These are line-item projects nominated by lawmakers for budget implementation, and they always have the corroboration, input, or influence of the legislator representing a particular constituency.[1] Despite the fact that legislators are only expected to recommend projects based on pressing needs of the people, they often use them as instead as pipes where the country's resources can be drained.

President Muhammadu Buhari, during the National Summit on Diminishing Corruption in the Public Sector in November of 2019, berated the National Assembly over the implementation of constituency projects, alleging that there is little to show for over N1 trillion budgeted for constituency projects of National Assembly members in the last ten years.[2] ICPC chairman Bolaji Owosanoye also disclosed at the induction of the Anti-Corruption and Transparency Unit of the Ministry of Environment in Abuja that issues brought to light by these initiatives include diversion, embezzlement of government funds, irregular payments, abuse of due process, budget padding, and unethical behavior in the workplace, pointing to the evidence that the commission recovered public funds amounting to over N9 billion from capital funds, plus N25.7 billion from personnel costs.[3]

Sadly, most Nigerian lawmakers are using their position to influence government agencies to manipulate the terms of contracts, which helps them divert funds meant for projects into their private use. Tonnie Iredia supports this position, saying that "although constituency projects are advertized as required by law, lawmakers have devised dubious ways of ensuring that only companies fronting for them or those belonging to the cronies are pre-qualified."[4] Owosanoye also indicted contractors, pointing out that some who were given allocations for this form of project failed to execute them, with others remaining poorly executed.[5]

Constituency Projects Tracking Group (CPTG), a task force of the ICPC, revealed how Nigerian lawmakers connive with agencies to embezzle billions of naira meant for constituency projects. The report, which is in its first phase, tracked 424 projects from the 2015–2018 ZIPs between June and August of 2019, covering 12 states - Adamawa, Akwa Ibom, Bauchi, Benue, Edo, Enugu, Imo, Kano, Kogi, Lagos, Osun and Sokoto - and the federal capital territory.[6] It disclosed duplication of some contracts that had the same description, same amount, and the same location awarded by the same agency.[7] The report stressed "This we found, is being done by the legislators in order to bring the total amount allocated to individual legislators within the approval threshold of the executing agency so as to avoid ministerial tender processes." One example cited is the project for the supply of eight tractors to Bauchi Central Senatorial Zone in 2016. This project, which allocated about N92 million, was split into four lots and awarded to three different contractors.[8]

ICPC also noticed that in the Small and Medium Enterprises Development Agency (SMEDAN) as well as the Border Communities Development Agency (BCDA), the size, number and types of ZIPs domiciled in the two agencies had turned them into conduits for abuse of constituency projects and therefore vulnerable to corruption.[9] The cost for constituency projects embedded as line items is sometimes far more than their allocation in the annual budget of these agencies. "For instance, in 2015, while the total mandate allocation for SMEDAN was N1,592,323,599, constituency projects allocation was N5,814,369,579."[10] Investigation by The Premium Times into the 2020 budget signed by the President Buhari revealed that not less than 20 agencies have their budget lines stuffed with projects which were 'sneaked' in by the legislators.[11] The online newspaper showed that these agencies' projects range from misplaced mandates to false location, with overpricing rampant.[12]

The following are the 20 agencies with their questionable projects for 2020 as presented by the Premium Times:

1. Federal Capital Territory Authority (FCTA)

The capital expenditure for the FCTA is N62.4 billion. More than half of this (N37 billion), instead of addressing Abuja's deplorable infrastructure, will go to fixing only the National Assembly Complex.

By comparison, all that is earmarked by the government for capital projects by the Federal Roads Maintenance Agency (FERMA) — the agency saddled with repairing broken federal roads across Nigeria — is N36.6 billion.

The money for the renovation of the parliament building is not part of the N128 billion voted for the National Assembly this year.

2. Universal Basic Education Commission

Premium Times' analysis shows how the N21.6 billion apportioned to UBEC would cater to a flurry of vague projects such as "supply of instructional materials to various schools in the North-east," priced at N500 million, the same price for the "supply of laptops and writing materials to schools in Borno State." Allocation to UBEC falls under the category of statutory transfers.

3. Office of the Senior Special Assistant to the President–MDGS (OSSAP-MDGS)

This office advises the President on how to eradicate poverty. It had an initial proposal of N34 million. However, in the new budget, the office has N5.1 billion.

The allocation is for the "supply of fertilisers, rice, maize and beans to Rano/Bunkuye Kibiya Federal Constituency, Kano State" with N250 million; "supply of goods, fertilisers rice, maize and beans in Katsina" and "supply of tricycles, motorcycles, sewing machines," each for N500 million; and "supply of new Toyota Hiace buses, utility vehicles SDG intervention," which would gulp N1.9 billion.

4. Border Communities Development Agency (BCDA)

Lawmakers raised BCDA's budget from the N3.7 billion proposed by President Buhari to N5.5 billion. The agency was founded to provide basic amenities to border communities in the country. In BCDA's appropriation for this year, however, N100 million is budgeted for "youth empowerment in Yobe East Senatorial District".

"Supply of tricycles and sewing machines in Yobe East Senatorial District" would take an additional N50 million.

5. Small and Medium Enterprise Development Agency of Nigeria (SMEDAN)

SMEDAN was established in 2003 to create an enabling environment for Small and Medium Scale Enterprises (SMSE) to thrive.

Premium Times found that its mandate has shifted because lawmakers made room for projects such as the "rehabilitation, surface dressing and construction of drainages of rural roads in selected locations in Isuiwato/Umunneochi federal constituency" for N500 million and "supply of mobile kiosks, mobile kitchen and modern SME tools entrepreneurial training for prospective entrepreneurs in Nigeria" for N730 million. About 200 more projects of this nature exist in the agency's budget.

6. Energy Commission of Nigeria (ECN)

ECN formulates and coordinates national policies on energy supply, based on the projects it has under its purview, but it should be focused more on implementation. It should be constructing a mini grid solar system for "small businesses" and "educational institutions" in selected LGAs, each for N1 billion.

This same agency, with N500 million, should provide street lights to the College of Education, Waka — the same items it should erect in Katsina South Senatorial District for N200 million. Finally, at N200 million each, it plans to construct solar boreholes in Lagos West, Niger East, Oyo North, and Central Senatorial Districts.

7. Nigeria Institute of Oceanography and Marine Research

Established in 1975 by the Research Institutes' Establishment Order, this institute has a mandate of conducting research on Nigeria's territorial waters. However, some of the projects it is supposed to oversee this year have nothing to do with research or with bodies of water at all.

It is supposed to grade an inner road in Alimosho for N300 million; supply chairs to schools in Oshodi, Isolo, Mushin, Ajeromi and Ojo for N100 million; erect solar street lights in some Lagos communities for N200 million; and construct town halls in six communities in Aniocha North, Aniocha South, Oshimili South, Oshimili North Federal Constituency, and Delta State (hometown of Hon. Ndudi Elumelu) for N285 million.

Likewise, aside from its plan to erect solar street lights in some Lagos communities for N200 million, it should also supply 200 units of Bajaj tricycles in Ikeja federal constituency for N200 million (N1 million each). A new Bajaj tricycle costs between N600,000 to N850,000.

Of the 45 projects domiciled under the institute, 31 are either empowerment or capacity building projects.

8. National Directorate of Employment (NDE)

NDE's budget was upped from N1.02 billion to approximately N14 billion. While its vision is said to be to create jobs for all, their budget appears to be for a flurry of empowerment projects that are difficult to track. Included is N550 million on "rural to urban mass transit empowerment programme in selected local government areas." It is also supposed to distribute "empowerment items to aspiring artisans and entrepreneurs" in all the six geopolitical zones of the country, each for N1 billion.

9. Nigeria Building and Road Research Institute (NBRRI)

Established April 1, 1978, NBRRI has a core mandate to conduct research on the building and construction sectors of the economy. Based on its projects for this year, however, it deviates from this mandate.

The budget passed and signed by the President has entrusted the institute with the responsibility to construct 20 kilometers of roads across all six geopolitical zones for N1.27 billion.

Also, with N1 billion, it should construct the Hauwadai Township road. This is notwithstanding its plan to construct classrooms in 11 locations in Plateau State for N80 million.

10. Project Development Institute, Enugu (PRODA)

PRODA should purchase tricycles in Anambra State for N350 million, and in Anambra North Senatorial District for N300 million. About 70 percent of its proposed projects are empowerment-based.

11. Nigerian Stored Products Research Institute (NSPRI), Ilorin

NSPRI, an agency headquartered in Ilorin whose job is to mitigate post-harvest loss of crops in Nigeria, plans to construct "ICT centres" and provide "equipment in selected secondary schools in Lagos." It is recorded that it will repeat this same project three times this year, all at a total cost of N768 billion — first for N255 million, then N256 million and N257 million.

NSPRI also has projects slated for Enugu, Niger, Delta and Rivers States, though save for the latter two, it does not have outstations in any of these. The outstations of the agency are located in Ibadan, Kano, Lagos, Maiduguri, Port-Harcourt, and Sapele. 80 percent of NSPRI's projects (55 of 68) are capacity-building and empowerment projects which ICPC advised should be suspended.

12. National Centre For Agricultural Mechanisation (NCAM)

With an eye on projects in the FCT, Kogi, and Oyo States, the NCAM plans to renovate "primary schools in selected areas in Lagos" for N475 million, rehabilitate "NTA Tejuosho–Railway Quarters Access Road", and install "solar street lights in Surulere" with N150 million.

Surulere is the constituency of Speaker of the House of Representatives Femi Gbajabiamila.

Not only does the Centre not have a branch in Lagos, it was established to "reduce drudgery and improve the quality of agricultural production and ensure food security for the nation."

70 percent of NCAM's projects (16 of 23) are empowerment projects.

13. Federal Cooperative College, Oji River

Rather than focusing on awarding diplomas in cooperative development courses, the Federal Cooperative College, Oji River is charged with procuring tricycles and with empowering women with cooperative society organisations in southeast Nigeria for N735 million.

Motorcycles should also be procured for "rural corporators" in Abia State with N800 million. Also in Abia State, the college plans to construct a 2 km road for N240 million and a 3 km road for the same amount.

Although it is located in Abia State, the college now has planned projects in Bauchi, Rivers, Anambra, Ebonyi and others.

14. Forestry Research Institute of Nigeria (FRIN)

A striking feature in the budget lines of this research institute is what it captures simply as "empowerment" for N50 million. No further details are provided.

Aside from projects it is meant to execute in each of Enugu, Gombe, Borno, Adamawa, Yobe, Kaduna, and Edo states, the Ibadan-based agency is to provide "laptops for students in selected secondary schools in both Coker Aguda and Itire Ikate, Surulere, Lagos" for N200 million.

The institute was supposedly formed to promote forestry development and environmental protection.

15. Federal College of Fisheries and Marine Technology, Lagos

This institution had N5.5 billion in its initial budget. About N1 billion of this was to be used to organise "empowerment training in boat operations and fishing for rural fishermen in Lagos West Senatorial District."

Ideally, it should be offering ordinary and higher diplomas to students in courses in fishery technology.

16-20. River Basin Development Authorities (RBDA)

Instead of shouldering the responsibility for managing water resources for agriculture and other uses, the River Basin

Development Authorities (RBDA) across the country are supposed to plan to construct roads and boreholes in 2021. There are 11 such agencies in the country.

The Lower Benue RBDA, for instance, apart from constructing roads "in selected locations in Wase, Plateau State," for N190 million should also construct roads "in selected locations in Plateau State" for N317.5 million.

Upper Niger RBDA also plans to construct a civic centre and shops in Niger North Senatorial District with N200 billion. Likewise, Sokoto Rima RBDA should spend N575 million on three rural roads in Zamfara State.

Analysis of the budget of Anambra/Imo RBDA also show that it is charged with construction of four solar-powered boreholes in Gombe South Senatorial District with N285 million. Meanwhile, the Ogun/Osun RBDA has a similar plan to construct solar street lights across Igboeze South LGA, Enugu State, with N150 million.[13]

BudgIT has also discovered frivolous and suspicious items embedded in the proposed 2019 budget that come with outrageous amounts attached. See below for a few examples:

Federal Ministry of Science and Technology
Line Item: Hosting of RIGAN Games
Cost: N118 million
Agency: Nigerian Building and Road Research Institute
Project Code: ERGP10116055

Federal Ministry of Information
Line Item: Grassroots Enlightenment Campaign on Government Policies & Program (including cost of production of materials and IEC on government achievements)
Cost: N190,722,680
Agency: Federal Ministry of Information and Culture
Project Code: ERGP9124022

Line Item: Nationwide Opinion Poll Survey on Government Policies and Programs
Cost: N100,179,709
Agency: Federal Ministry of Information and Culture
Project Code: ERGP9124028

Federal Ministry of Women Affairs

Line Item: Nationwide Advocacy and Sensitization Activities
Cost: N140 million
Agency: Federal Ministry of Women Affairs
Project Code: ERGP22112040

Line Item: Nationwide Advocacy and Sensitization Activities
Cost: N140,000,000
Agency: Federal Ministry of Women Affairs
Project Code: ERGP22112040

Ministry of Budget and National Planning

Line Item: Special Intervention (Recurrent)
Cost: N350 billion
Agency: Service Wide Vote
Project Code: ERGP1115526

Line Item: Presidential Enabling Business Environment Council (PEBEC)
Cost: N500 million
Agency: Service Wide Vote
Project Code: ERGP1132717

Line Item: Galaxy backbone
Cost: N4 billion
Agency: Service Wide Vote
Project Code: ERGP29115486

Federal Ministry of Science and Technology

Line Item: Completion and Equipping of Garri Processing Plant in Atani, Abia State
Cost: N100 million
Agency: Federal Institute of Industrial Research, Oshodi
Project Code: ERGP30128993

Line Item: Advocacy & Publication for Job Creation
Cost: N100,499,994
Agency: Federal Institute of Industrial Research, Oshodi
Project Code: ERGP113296

Line Item: Pan African Tsetse and Trypanosomiasis Eradication Campaign
Cost: N85 million
Agency: Nigerian Institute for Trypanosomiasis Research, Kaduna
Project Code: ERGP1108265

Federal Ministry of Interior

Line Item: Promotion and Discipline
Cost: N22,080,945
Agency: Civil Defense, Immigration, and Prison Service Board (CIPB)
Project Code: ERGP16126527.[14]

A lot of lawmakers hide under the cloak of empowerment programs to loot the country dry because such projects are difficult to track. Most of the funds voted for them seldom get to the intended beneficiaries. For instance, N23,750,000 was voted for a project described as the Strategic Empowerment for Women in Okitipupa/Irele Federal Constituency, Ondo State. Tracka found out and reported on Twitter that about 100 beneficiaries were selected, trained, and received N20,000 as start-up capital.[15] The paltry sum distributed to beneficiaries pales in comparison to the N23.7 million allotted for the project. Another instance is when

N25 million was allocated for the supply of motorcycles to youths in Funtua/Dandume Federal Constituency in Katsina State. Tracka reported that 30 motorcycles were given to selected beneficiaries including police and NDLEA personnel, and labeled as donation.[16]

The bottom line is that some lawmakers are just there to plunder public wealth at the slightest opportunity. Cases abound whereby lawmakers seize an opportunity. When projects are approved for constituents, they use them to enrich themselves. For instance, in August of 2019, the ICPC recovered items worth N117 million which were stashed away in a compound in Mkpologu Town that was believed to be owned by the Senator Chukwuka Utazi.[17] The agency explained that the tricycles, motorcycles, and grinding machines recovered were meant to be distributed to Utazi's constituents, to empower them as part of the federal government's efforts to alleviate poverty.[18] A statement signed by ICPC spokesperson Rasheedat Okoduwa said that the contract for purchase of the items was awarded on January 23, 2018, as part of Utazi's constituency projects.[19]

In another example, N430 million was awarded in 2015 for the supply of pumping machines and other agricultural machinery to farmers in Bauchi Central Senatorial District as part of Senator Isa Misau's constituency projects. The CPTG team for Bauchi discovered that N76.6 million was paid for the tractors in December 2015, but they were only supplied in March of 2016. They were supposed to have been distributed for the use of farmers in each of the six local government areas in the senatorial district that included Misau, Dambam, Ningi, Warji, Darazo and Ganjuwa. But it was found that the tractors had not been distributed as required in the terms of the contract.[20]

In fact, situations similar to the aforementioned cases have occured routinely over the years in different parts of the country. According to Eno-Abasi Sunday, "these glaring breaches have also succeeded in making the initiative one of the most notorious corrupt schemes since the return of democracy in 1999."[21]

The legislature should have been a major barrier against corruption in Nigeria because of its oversight function in probing cases of malpractice in the public sector. But as this arm of government seems badly blighted by the virus of corruption, it is clear that tackling said corruption could be an effort in futility. Recall the "Otedollar" saga when Lawan Farouk, a legislator acclaimed for integrity, the head of the House Ad-Hoc Committee to Verify and Determine the Actual Subsidy Requirements, was exposed by Femi Otedola for receiving $620,000 of a $3 million bribe to facilitate the removal of the names of his (Otedola's) two indicted companies from the list of oil marketers set to be sanctioned for receiving millions of dollars for oil imports that were not made.

To further confirm the National Assembly as a cesspool of corruption, Senator Godswill Akpabio, Minister of the Niger Delta Affairs, linked some members of the Assembly to high level corruption at the NDDC during a public hearing in July of 2020. He alleged that lawmakers are the greatest beneficiaries of questionable NDCC contracts, a situation that prompted the House Committee chairman, Thomas Ereyitomi, to request that Senator Akpabio should "off the mic."

If the legislature's credibility is compromised to this extent, how can it curtail the corrupt excesses of the executive and, by extension, the judiciary branch? It is common knowledge that legislators who soil their hands in constituency project scams are careful not to press too hard to avoid being exposed. This shows that victory over corruption will continue to be elusive.

CHAPTER SIX

Half Justice Better Than None

In traditional Nigerian society, the penalty for stealing can be incredibly severe no matter how insignificant the stolen items are. The punishment ranges from a beating right up to killing the suspect, as the case may be. In most places in the south, suspects are often maimed, paraded naked through markets, town squares, and other public places, and might even be burned to death. In northern Nigeria, the penalty for theft might be amputation of the limbs or execution by guillotine or by stoning.

In Nigerian traditional society, the punishment for stealing is severe purposefully, to deter others from committing similar acts in the future. While some places may opt for milder punitive measures, the accused might still be completely banished from the community. Apart from stealing within the family - which might attract mild punishment - theft outside the home is a crime against the public, and it often compels mob action. This form of instant punishment is sometimes referred to as jungle justice, and it has persisted from pre-colonial days to contemporary times.

In the Aluu Four incident, Lloyd Toku, Ugonna Obuzor, Tekena Elkannah and Chiadika Biringa were young male undergraduates who were burned to death on October 5, 2012 in the Aluu community of Rivers State. They were accused of robbery, but it was later confirmed in court that they were not actually guilty. As barbaric and condemnable as jungle justice might be, it does point to the fact that Nigerians do not tolerate it when individuals convert money or items belonging to others to their own use.

It is, however, paradoxical that Nigerians have zero tolerance to petty theft while the massive looting of public funds continues with impunity. Surprisingly, people seem to celebrate the corrupt political leaders who plunder the government treasury. A good example is when the people of Oghara, including policemen, thronged the residence of the former Delta State governor James Ibori in February of 2017 with pomp and fanfare to welcome him home after he was released from jail in Britain. According to Premium Times, "Hundreds of people marched round the town carrying leaves while some painted their faces with chalk. Musical bands entertained the crowd at various points."[1] Ighoyota Amori, a former senator representing Delta Central, said the return of Ibori was a good omen to the people.[2] He said, "We are happy that Ibori is back, people are jubilating, the crowd you see here and the enthusiasm that has been displayed today showed that we really missed him."[3]

Tafa Balogun, who was convicted and jailed for six months for stealing and laundering billions of naira from 2002 to 2004 while he was the inspector general of police, was in November 2020 conferred with the traditional chieftaincy title of Oluomo of Igbominaland, an award of excellence in the ancient town of Ila-Orangun in Osun State. Another instance is when the former Bayelsa State governor Diepreye Alamieyeseigha was warmly received as a folk hero by a mammoth crowd in his hometown after dressing as a woman, faking a passport, and skipping bail in Britain following charges for laundering £1.8 million. There is also the case of Bode George as recounted by Human Rights Watch, "When ruling party chieftain Olabode George emerged from prison in 2011 after serving a two-and-a-half year sentence following a landmark EFCC prosecution, he was treated to a rapturous welcome by members of Nigeria's political elite including former president Obasanjo and then-defense minister, Ademola Adetokunbo."[4] It is a stunning truth that those who steal big from the public coffers are celebrated to high heavens by the masses, while those who steal food in order to satiate their hunger receive instant jungle justice.

In Nigeria, stealing on a grand scale seems to attract inconsequential punitive measures. A look at some of the rulings on corruption cases shows that Nigeria's zeal to stamp out corruption is naught but a mockery. There are numerous instances of minimal penalties being meted out despite the magnitude of the crimes. For example, high court judge Abubakar Talba handed a two year jail term with a N250,000 fine option to John Yakubu Yusuf, a former assistant director in the federal civil service, in 2013. Yusuf was one of the six federal officials tried for stealing N32.8 billion from the police pension fund. His sentencing came after Yusuf pled guilty to fraudulently converting N2 billion of police pension funds to private use. Much to the chagrin of observers, the accused was let go with the option to avoid his jail term by submitting to a comparatively slight payment of N250 thousand.

Lucky Igbinedion, former governor of Edo State, was charged with stealing up to N4.4 billion. But in a high court ruling in Enugu, Igbinedion was fined a paltry N3.5 million with no option of jail time for over eight years of looting the Edo State treasury.[5] In a comical replay of the same episode, Lucky Igbinedion's younger brother Michael, who was being prosecuted by the EFCC for siphoning N25 billion from the Edo State treasury while his elder brother held power, was convicted and received a fine of N3 million from Justice J. Liman of the Federal High Court in Benin.[6]

Tafa Balogun, despite being arraigned at the Federal High Court in Abuja for stealing and laundering over $100 million in his three years as inspector general of police,[7] was directed by Judge Binta Nyako to pay N500,000 on each of the eight charges while also receiving just six months of imprisonment following a plea bargain.[8]

After eight years of prosecution of Danjuma Goje for perpetrating an alleged N25 billion in fraud while serving as Gombe State governor, the EFCC surprisingly quashed 19 of the 21 counts in 2019, a day after Goje met with President Buhari and agreed to cede his quest for the Senate presidency. The attorney general applied for the withdrawal of the two remaining corruption charges against Goje in 2019, and the case died.[9]

A lot of corruption cases have been murdered in the courts on technicalities. A clear example is the case of Senator Orji Uzor Kalu, the chief whip representing Abia North. Kalu was convicted in December of 2019 over allegations of fraud worth N7.65 billion committed while he was governor of Abia State from 1999 to 2007. Justice Idris Mohammed sentenced him to 12 years in prison, finding him guilty of defrauding the Abia State government through his company Slok Nigeria Limited. After spending six months in jail, his sentence was overturned by the Supreme Court on the basis that the judge who sentenced him had been elevated to the Court of Appeal at the time of the judgment, and hence had no authority to deliver it.[10] It was said that this meant he lacked jurisdiction to conduct the trial.[11] Although the court did not acquit him, it did order a retrial of the former governor.[12] While the EFCC says it will take Senator Kalu to court for retrial, the case might actually never see the light of day.

The Nation Newspaper, in its June 26, 2014 editorial, lamented how the commission's probing of high-profile individual cases, mostly involving alleged corrupt public officers, continue endlessly without any commendable denouement, with many dogged by dull-witted and convoluted procedures that drag on endlessly.[13] As rightfully noted by Prof. Bolaji Owasanoye, the EFCC has always pointed to the slow judicial process as an obstacle to quick determination of some of its cases.[14] "Its position, which represents a partial truth, is that it cannot play the role of prosecutor and judge. Once a case is filed, the Chief/Administrative Judge concerned has the discretionary power to assign the case to any court of his choice. Thereafter, both the counsels to the Commission and accused are at the mercy of the trial judge. Although many of the judges are working under very unfavorable conditions to dispense justice, few others rely on technicalities to defeat justice."[15] Ibori's case serves as an eye-opener. When questioned by international media, how does one explain that a Nigerian court cleared this ex-governor of Delta

State of several charges of mind-blowing acts of corruption – on grounds that he had no case to answer – when he was easily prosecuted, convicted, and sentenced to 13 years by a British court on similar charges?[16]

Nothing kills a good corruption case in Nigeria as well as delays. Justice delayed, it is said, is justice denied, and courts have fast become the worst place to get justice as corruption cases are deliberately frustrated and prolonged by lawyers. According to a Human Rights Watch report, "most of the EFCC's cases against nationally prominent political figures have been stalled in the courts for years without the trials even commencing. Nigeria's weak and overburdened judiciary offers seemingly endless opportunities for skilled defense lawyers to secure interminable and sometimes frivolous delays."[17]

As reported in The Nation Newspaper in May 2016, the trial of Saminu Turaki, former governor of Jigawa State, had been lingering for nine years due to application of delays.[18] The EFCC had to raid the former governor's residence in Abuja to execute the warrant of arrest after he neglected to present himself for trial at the Federal High Court in Dutse in connection to N36 billion he allegedly stole while in office.[19]

Prof. Bolaji Owasanoye observes that most corruption trials in Nigeria suffer delays in court because they follow a predictable pattern. The trend is as follows:

1.   Grand arrest and arraignment, usually with proliferated charges running into hundreds of counts.
2.   Accused pleads "not guilty" and is admitted to bail with concomitant judicial order that international passports be deposited with the court.
3.   Once the accused gets bail, the game begins. The accused may first challenge the jurisdiction of the court even though the

matter of jurisdiction is well settled by a long line of cases decided by the Supreme Court.

4.   If challenge to jurisdiction fails (as it often does) and the court proceeds with the case, a number of steps may be taken by the defense such as:

· Appealing the ruling on jurisdiction immediately; or

· Applying to transfer the case from the judge on grounds of bias; or

· Applying to change defense counsel in order to gain time;

· The newly changed defense counsel immediately requests adjournment to study the file;

· Case enters period of incessant adjournments which ultimately takes it away from the radar of the media and public attention;

5.   After a brief lull, the defense files an application for release of the accused's international passport to travel overseas for medical or religious reasons;

6.   Court grants the application for release of passport, sometimes without interrogating the propriety of the reasons; for example, the court hardly considers the number of adjournments of defense that have delayed the case thus far;

7.   Further delay follows the release of the passport;

8.   If any of these applications is overruled, a long appeal process follows;

9.   The likelihood of the trial proceeding on substantive grounds gradually wanes and may eventually be extinguished as witnesses recant, lose memory, or become inconsistent in testimony;

10. Defense may begin a campaign of bias, persecution, political trial, etc. against prosecuting agency;

11. Prosecuting agency also begins to display signs of fatigue, frustration, or even complicity;

12. Public and media apathy follows. The public no longer expects justice and may begin to accuse the prosecuting agency of incompetence, bias, or other complicity.

13. Eventually the case may be struck for want of prosecution, or the accused is eventually set free.[20]
The above pattern can be discerned in the case of Dr. Chimaroke Nnamani, the former governor of Enugu State.

Nnamani was first arraigned before Justice Abubakar Tijani in 2007, but three judges handled the trial before it was transferred to Justice Mohammed Yinusa. In April 2013, the judge granted Nnamani leave to travel overseas for medical treatment. His lawyer told the court that he was suffering from hypercholesterolemia, a condition characterized by very high levels of cholesterol in the blood. The former governor's overseas trip led to court adjournment twice: first in May and then in September of 2013 because the accused had not returned.[21] When the matter came up again on May 4, 2014, his defense counsel asked for another adjournment, arguing that the matter was for mention rather than hearing. The judge conceded, notwithstanding objection by the prosecuting counsel, and further adjourned the case to June 17, 2014.[22]

Besides the antics and tactics of delays, the judges themselves are overworked. This factor conspires a great deal to create extraordinary delays in concluding corruption trials. Hadizatu Uwani Mustapha, the second female and 17th Chief Registrar of the Supreme Court, stressed in an interview for This Day Newspaper that justices are overburdened with frivolous appeals that should not be clogging their dockets. "From 2007-2019 alone, we have about 10,000 appeals pending," she says. "The Honourable Justices of the Supreme Court of Nigeria are the most overworked Justices of any Supreme Court in the entire globe."[23]

This situation, indeed, is a major clog that makes the wheel of justice in Nigeria grind slowly.
Timely and swift dispensation of justice could have served resounding penalties on those convicted of graft. Such penalties

might even deter them from committing further financial crimes, while making the public conscious that certain offences will, in fact, be punished. This deterrence factor is what contributes to reducing the probability of certain offenses. The core reason traditional societies in Nigeria roast thieves to death or amputate them is to incentivize deterrence and to forewarn others that they will meet a similar fate if they steal. Because of the deterrence exuded by jungle justice, most people stay away from stealing.

Conversely, in Nigeria, the judiciary is found wanting in dispensing justice capable of deterring individuals and organizations from stealing from the coffers of government. The situation is so bad that the only time the alleged offenders are disturbed is when they are arrested by anti-graft agencies and incarcerated until the court grants them bail. When litigation begins, it continues for years at a snail's pace. When conviction eventually comes, the culprit receives a very light penalty despite the high magnitude of the financial crimes committed.

How on earth could a judge hand a two-year jail term, with a paltry fine option of N250,000, to John Yakubu Yusuf after he stole N2 billion in police pension funds? How could Tafa Balogun walk away with over $100 million, receiving only a six-month jail sentence and a fine of N4 million? Is it not astounding that Lucky Igbinedion, who stole up to N4.4 billion, could be allowed to go free, parting with a paltry N3.5 million fine, with no option of jail term? The same goes for Igbinedion's brother Michael. After he stole N25 billion from the Edo State treasury, he received just a N3 million fine. This is half justice. It is as good as putting no punitive measures in place because it cannot deter others from plundering wealth belonging to the state. Politicians go haywire, fleecing the state of financial resources while knowing full well that if they cannot delay justice until it fizzles, the penalty will be light - just a slap on the wrist - after which they will regain their freedom and live in peace to enjoy their bounty.

A lot of perpetrators of corrupt practices are walking free and enjoying their loot because of the defective Nigerian judicial system. They openly display their ill-gotten wealth in the midst of mass poverty. It is such an irony of society that Nigerians cannot tolerate petty thieves but will turn around to worship those who loot their country's treasuries dry. The trend has inspired ambitious individuals to fancy corruption as a shortcut to material prosperity. Given this situation, is there any hope that corruption will ever end?

CHAPTER SEVEN

Conclusion: No End On The Horizon

Olusegun Adeniyi, an ace journalist and former spokesperson for President Yar'Adua, recounts his experience with former Delta State governor James Ibori, who was enmeshed in a corruption scandal at the time: "I recall the day Ibori came to my office to warn me, he said something very instructive: "Look Segun, there is nowhere in the world where you help somebody to power, and his reward for you is that you go to jail. It doesn't happen anywhere, and it won't begin with me"[1]

Of course politicians help themselves to power. Once they are in power, they set their eyes on gains, nothing short of that. If Ibori helped Yar'Adua to power, it means he was part of the winning team and he would not expect to be thrown off board. Leaving him in jail would have gone against the political morality of a country overtaken by widespread graft.

The reason that the war against corruption in Nigeria will never be won, amongst other considerations, is that those who install leaders expect to be rewarded with nothing less than access to the state's great wealth. Those who are part of the winning team are sacred cows; their past sins are often forgiven. This could have been the reason Ibori's corruption case was thrown out in Nigeria, while he was tried and convicted for the same case abroad. When the EFCC brought 170 criminal counts against Ibori, a judge sitting in Ibori's home state threw out every single count, including evidence that Ibori paid EFCC officials $15 million in an attempt to influence the outcome of the investigation.[2] It was only in Britain that the long arm of the law caught up with James Ibori. Yar'Adua's government, which Ibori had helped install, could not have allowed him to reap tribulation instead of wholesome reward. Stakeholders and members of a ruling party do not see looting of public funds as an act of corruption. They see it, rather, as a way of reaping what they sowed, having brought their party to power. After all, it is their time to control and share the national cake. Eating from the government they sweated to form is no wrongdoing, but instead a reward. In this way, only partisan affiliation can determine who faces prosecution and conviction and who does not.

During a political rally in Benin prior to 2019 general elections, Adams Oshiomole, former national chairman of the All Progressives Congress (APC), was heard urging corrupt members of the opposition Peoples' Democratic Party (PDP) to join APC so that their sins could be forgiven. He said, "We have some PDP defectors. They are, Henry Tenebe, Iluobe….Iluobe means I have done something wrong. Yes, once you join the APC, your sins are forgiven."[3]

No, corruption will not be rooted out in Nigeria's body politic. It will continue to remain intractable. As long as the game of politics remains an avenue for power and for the acquisition of governmental positions and distribution of state's wealth, all 11 out of 10 politicians will continue to control the system with a culture of corruption. They will dictate the direction and pace the government should take, just for their own interest.

The concept that 11 out of 10 politicians are corrupt, as puzzling as that sounds, is simply an adoption of the soccer formation approach to explain that politicians are the 10 outfield players. They do not pass the ball amongst themselves alone, but they also pass to the goalie who is player 11. The 11th player, in our metaphor, could be in the judiciary, be a business mogul, a contractor, a friend, a family member, etc. Pressure that forces office holders to steal from the coffers of the government usually comes from the vast social networks to which the politicians belong. According to Ngozi Okonjo-Iweala, "if people believe that the purpose of obtaining office is to provide one's family and friends with money, goods, favors, or appointments, then social networks can perpetuate the norm of corruption."[4]

Nurudeen Alliyu of Olabisi Onabanjo University identifies key beneficiaries of corruption in a social network in the table that follows:

S/N	The Eaters	Mode of Eating
1.	Traditional Institutions	Traditional titles to federal/state/local government; official courtesy visits at government houses
2.	Religious Institutions	Prayer Mercantilism; thanksgiving and spiritual blessings
3.	Legal Institutions	Judicial manipulations and outright judgment purchase
4.	Educational Institutions	Awards carefully wrapped in public lectures
5.	Family Institutions	Birthdays, festivals, and ceremonies
6.	Civil Societies	Public appearances, lectures, and rallies
7.	Unions/Associations	Courtesy visits, lectures, and rallies
8.	Professional Bodies	Courtesy visits and subtle demand of the impossible from their excellencies
9.	Media Business Patronage	Advertisements, media meetings with their excellencies, media awards of 'excellence'
10.	Ethnic Nationalities	Threats and acts of public disturbances; amnesty, etc.
11.	Security Agencies	Security meetings with their excellencies, 'securing the communities, people, life and property'
12.	Political Institutions	Inflated contracts; political conflicts/gatherings/meetings; courtesy calls and ceremonies of their excellencies and notable politicians
13.	International Collaborators	Buyers of stolen crude artifacts and other items from Nigeria

Corruption and the Eaters of Corrupt Proceeds[5]

Political leaders' urge to steal and to give statutory entitlements will always be there. They will meet the needs of political backgrounders because they do not want to lose popularity and relevance.

Another reason corruption will not be stamped out in Nigeria is because it permeates all organs of government and checks any meaningful threat to its existence. The three arms of corruption as embedded in the executive, legislative, and judiciary organs are all playing complementary roles to help powerful elites in government enrich themselves and dominate the majority of citizens.

With three arms of corruption in place, war against graft can never be won in Nigeria. How do three arms of corruption operate to prevent such a win? First, the executive branch comes out with initiatives that ostensibly serve the public good though in reality drain public finances; they siphon funds meant for the projects, programs and policies to private use. They eschew due process to benefit themselves at the expense of the majority.

The legislative branch, who are supposed to probe corrupt activities of the executives, are found neck-deep in contract scams involving constituency projects. To avoid being exposed in constituency project scams, they seal their lips and play along with corrupt elements in the executive arm. Sometimes they stage-manage investigations and at times shelve their findings. If the matter goes to court, then it becomes easy for the corrupt to manipulate the Nigerian judiciary, circumventing the laws and getting away with the loot. Prof. Mamman Lawan of Bayero University says bribing judges is an investment for politicians, which they intend to recoup with huge profits when public resources come to their disposal.[6]

As long as Nigeria's judiciary system is defective and corrupt, its handling of corruption matters will not create any meaningful impact on the anti-corruption fight. Since the judiciary is so recklessly corrupt, then Nigeria should forget about exiting the web of corruption anytime soon. According to a report by ICPC's Anti-Corruption Academy of Nigeria, the justice sector between 2018 and 2020 had the highest level of corruption with a score of 63. The executive and legislative sectors had overall corruption scores of 42 and 41 respectively.[7] If the judiciary is this corrupt, then Nigeria is in a pathetic situation.

With corruption spreading through all three organs of government, Nigeria's version of democracy is just a perversion that benefits the minority who form the political class while the majority of common people practically live in negligence. The dividends of democracy that ought to benefit the majority have been hijacked by the powerful few. Abubakar Tsav, former commissioner of the police in Lagos, spoke to the Vanguard in November 2019, lamenting the extent to which Nigeria's democracy has degenerated: "Our democracy is turning into something else. We seem not to know what democracy even means. Many see it as a means to acquire wealth albeit by fraudulent and dishonest means… The fight against corruption has no impact on our people and that is why politicians are still fighting and killing themselves for elective offices."[8]

A judiciary system that cannot dispense justice capable of deterring people from further indulgence in corruption shows us that triumph over corruption is not still within reach. As the wheels of justice keep grinding slowly, there can never be any impact in a fight against corruption. Dr. Esa Onoja, a senior lecturer at the Nigerian Law School in Abuja, revealed during a public presentation in April 2018 that the nation's two anti-graft agencies, EFCC and ICPC, secured only ten high profile convictions in 17 years, and that out of the ten high profile convictions, only three went to full trial.[9] This record of convictions is a far cry from the actual amount of financial crimes that are committed over such a period of time. This also shows that Nigeria has a long way to go in winning the war against corruption.

As long as principal officials in the judiciary are appointed by politicians in the executive, it is hard to rule out the possibility of favoritism, nepotism, or appointments for political gain. For instance, the Chief Justice of Nigeria emerges by the nomination of the President upon recommendation by the National Judicial

Council, which is further subject to confirmation by the Nigerian Senate. Similarly, the appointments of high court judges are made by the governor upon recommendation by the National Judicial Council. In all, the manner in which justices are appointed makes the entire process more susceptible to cynical manipulation in order to suit the whims and caprices of the corrupt political class. This automatically undermines the independence of the judiciary because politicians eagerly seize the privilege to maneuver the system in order to stay afloat.

Back in 2013, Justice Amina Augie condemned this system during the Nigerian Bar Association's annual conference in Calabar: "We have the political situation that has thrown up all manner of persons as judges… We now have a situation where politicians, who would want a way to compensate their girlfriends and man friends, nominate them for appointment as judges. And when they are so appointed, they become a problem to the judiciary… These judges hide under every kind of pretext to adjourn matters or even strike out cases."[10]

It is a sad situation. Nigeria really needs an independent judiciary able to dispense justice accordingly no matter whose ox is gored. There must be judicial reform. International agreement on judicial appointment should be followed, and appointments should be made on merit and based on criteria pre-established by law or by competent authorities, with political considerations being inadmissible (UNODC, 2015, para. 53-55; GA Resolution 40/32 and 40/146, para. 10 and 13).[11] The criteria should be brought to the public, and members of the law profession should be made aware of vacancies and recruitment exercises for the appointment and elevation of judges. Those persons who meet the criteria should be directed to apply.

There should also be special courts designated for corruption cases, with matters given accelerated hearing. Funding of the courts should be independent of the executive arm in order to avoid manipulation of judges. The EFCC Act should be amended to create a provision that will prevent interlocutory applications on EFCC cases from going beyond the Court of Appeal.

Finally, civil society organizations and the media should also play a part in naming and shaming judges, lawyers, and political office holders who conspire with the accused to frustrate Nigeria's untenable level of corruption.

ENDNOTES

Chapter 01

[1]Zahid, Muhammad (14 February 2015). "Who Gets What, When and How?" The Nation >
https://nation.com.pk/14-feb-2015 /who-gets-what-when-and-how

[2]Ogundiya, Ilufoye (2009). "Political Corruption in Nigeria: Theoretical Perspectives and Some Explanations" in: Anthropologist, 11(4). Sokoto: Department of Political Science, Usmanu Danfodiyo University, Sokoto, p.282.

[3]Ibid.p.283.

[4]Ibid.

[5] Lewis, Peter (1999). Nigeria's economy: Opportunity and challenge (vol. 27, no. 1), p. 53.

[6]Ekukanma, Tochukwu (8 July 2019). "Nigeria: What Manner of Democracy?" in: The Nation, p.17.

[7] Adisa, Olufemi (August 2019). "Nigerian Government and Governance- Democracy Or Kleptocracy?" in: Journal of Good Governance and Sustainable Development in Africa (JGGSDA) (Vol. 4, No 4) p.35.

[8]Igwe, S.C. (2010). How Africa Underdeveloped Africa. Port Harcourt: Professional Printers & Publishers, p.99.

[9]Ibid.

[10]UNODC. "Nigeria's Corruption Busters". unodc.org>
https://www.unodc.org/unodc/en/frontpage/nigerias-corruption-busters.html

[11]Mustapha, Mala (July2010). "Corruption in Nigeria: Conceptual & Empirical Notes" in: Information, Society & Justice (Vol. 3, No. 2). London: Department of Applied Social Sciences, London Metropolitan University, p. 169.

[12]Human Rights Watch (2007). "Criminal Politics, Violence, 'Godfathers' and Corruption in Nigeria" (vol. 19, no. 16) (A): New York.

[13]Bellanaija.com (30 March 2018). "FG lists Names of Looters, PDP Kicks" >
https://www.bellanaija.com/2018/03/fg-looters-pdp-kicks/

[14]Ibid.

[15]Premiumtimesng.com (1 April 2018). "Nigerian Govt Releases More Names of Alleged Looters" >
https://www.premiumtimesng.com/news/headlines/263724-nigerian-govt-releases-more-names-of-alleged-looters.html

[16]Ibid.

[17]Tahir, Tahir I. (8 July 2019). "An Amnesty Programme for Corruption?" in: The Nation Newspaper, p. 32.

[18]Ibid.

Chapter 02

[1]Uya, Okon (2005). African Diaspora. Calabar: Clear Lines Publications, p.69.

[2]Ibid.

[3]Ibid.

[4]Ibid., p.68.

[5]Ekong, Ekong (2001). Sociology of the Ibibio: A study of Social Organization and Change. Uyo: Modern Business Press Ltd., p.142.

[6]Uya, Okon (2005). African Diaspora, pp.66-67.

[7]Ibid.

[8]Ibid., p.66.

[9]Ibid., p.67.

[10]Dike, Kenneth (1956). Trade and Politics in the Niger-Delta.

[11]Uya, Okon (2005). African Diaspora, p.66.

[12]Ibid., p.68.

[13]Akpan, Otoabasi (2004). "The Evolution of the Nigerian State: Pre-colonial to Independence Period" in: Akpan, Akpan & Abiodun Oluwabamide (eds.). Nigerians and Their Cultural Heritage. Lagos: Lisjohnson Resources Publishers, p.14.

[14]Ikime, O. (1982). The Fall of Nigeria: The British Conquest. London: Heinemann Books, p.7.

[15]Akpan, Otoabasi (2004). "The Evolution of the Nigerian State: Pre-colonial to Independence Period" in: Akpan, Akpan & Abiodun Oluwabamide (eds.). Nigerians and Their Cultural Heritage, p.14.

[16]Ikime, O. (1982) The Fall of Nigeria: The British Conquest, p.7.

[17] Umoh, B.E. (1981). Corruption: A Social Concern In Nigeria. Uyo: Renson Press.
[18]Ibid.

[19]Akpan, Uwem (2016). "A Historical Overview of Corruption in Nigeria: 1856-1966" in Umoette, Godwin (ed.). Journal of Public Governance and Administration (Vol.1, No.1.). Uyo: Department of Political Science & Public Administration, University of Uyo, p.34.

[20]Ibid.

[21]Ibid.

[22]Ibid.

[23]Ibid.

[24]Ayandele, E. A. (1964). The Missionary Impact on Modern Nigeria. London: Longman, Green and Co.

[25]Akpan, Uwem (2016). "A Historical Overview of Corruption in Nigeria: 1856-1966" in Umoette, Godwin (ed.). Journal of Public Governance and Administration (Vol.1, No.1.), p.35.

[26]Ibid.

[27]Aluko, J.O. (2006). Corruption in the Local Government System in Nigeria. Ibadan: BookBuilders.

[28]Agedah, D. (ed.) (1993). Corruption and the Stability of the Third Republic. Lagos: Perception Communications.

[29]Akpan, Uwem (2016). "A Historical Overview of Corruption in Nigeria: 1856-1966" in: Journal of Public Governance and Administration (Vol.1, No.1.), p.36.

[30]Uwanaka, C.U. (1982). Zik and Awo in Colonial Storm. Lagos: Daily Times Press, p.34.

[31]Ojiako, J.O. (1981). "Nigeria: Yesterday, Today, And…" Onitsha: Africana Educational Publishers.

[32]Agedah, D. (ed.) (1993). Corruption and the Stability of the Third Republic.

[33]Sklar, R.L. (1963). Nigerian Political Parties, Power in an Emergent African State. New York: Nok Publishers.
[34]Akpan, Uwem (2016). "A Historical Overview of Corruption in Nigeria: 1856-1966," p.36.

[35]Ibid.

[36]Ibid.

[37]Egbe, B.O. and E.C. Ihejiamaizu (2001). The Sociology of Traditional and Modern Political Administrative Systems and Some Contentious Issues in Contemporary Nigeria. Calabar: Africana Scholars Publishing Company.

[38]Ademoyega, A. (1981). Why We Struck. Evans: Ibadan, p.14.

[39]Elaigwu, J.I. (2009). Scholarly Biography of a Soldier Statesman. Jos: Aha Publishing House Ltd., p. 367.

[40]Shehu Musa Yar'Adua Foundation (2004). Shehu Musa Yar'Adua: A Life of Service. Abuja, p.102.

[41] Agedah, D. (ed.) (1993). Corruption and the Stability of the Third Republic. Lagos: Perception Communications, pp.28-29.

[42]Akpan, Uwem (2015). "Corruption Under Military Regimes in Nigeria: 1966-1999" in: Inegbe, Stephen (ed.). The Parnassus: University of Uyo Journal of Cultural Research (Vol. 11), p.39.

[43]Ibid., p.44.

[44]Ibid.

[45]Mohammed, Aliyu et al (2018). "Corruption And Materialism: A Bane For Good Governance And Development In Nigeria" in: Nigerian Journal Of Social Studies (Vol. XXI (1)). Maru: Department of Social Studies, Zamfara State College of Education, p.244.

[46]Ogbeidi, M. M. (2012). Political Leadership And Corruption In Nigeria Since 1960: A Socio-Economic Analysis. Journal of Nigeria Studies: 1 (2). Retrieved from http://www.unh.edu/nigerianstudies/articles/Issue2/Political_leadership.pdf

[47] Ibid.

[48]Gboyega, A. (1996). Corruption and Democratization in Nigeria. Ibadan: Agbo Areo Publishers.

[49]Akpan, Uwem (2015). "Corruption Under Military Regimes in Nigeria: 1966-1999" in: The Parnassus: University of Uyo Journal of Cultural Research (Vol. 11), p.46.

[50]Ibid., pp.46-47.

[51]Ibid., p.47.

[52]Mamadu, T.T. (2009). Corruption in the Leadership Structure of Nigerian Polity. Calabar: Jocchrisam Publishers.

[53]Eminue, O. (2006). Military in Politics. Uyo: Soulmate Press and Publishers.

[54]Okonjo-Iweala (2018). Fighting Corruption is Dangerous: The Story Behind the Headlines. Cambridge, MA: The MIT Press, p.69.

[55]Adeniyi, Olusegun (2005). The Last 100 Days of Abacha: Political Drama in Nigeria Under One of Africa's Most Corrupt And Brutal Military Dictatorships. Lagos: The Bookhouse Company, p.xv.

[56]Ibid., p.xvi.

[57]Onyeka-Ben, V. (1999). "A President's Will to Bark and Bite" in: The Guardian, 30 June.

[58]Akpan, Uwem (2015). "Corruption Under Military Regimes in Nigeria: 1966-1999" in: The Parnassus: University of Uyo Journal of Cultural Research (Vol. 11), p.50.

[59]Ibid., p.51.

[60]Eminue, O. (2006). Military in Politics, p.528.

[61]Oshewolo, Segun & J. Olanrewaju (2011). "From Hell: The Surge of Corruption in Nigeria (1999 – 2007)" in: Academic Leadership: The Online Journal (Vol. 9). Retrieved from https://core.ac.uk/download/pdf/214523024.pdf.

[62]Fashola M. A. (2016). "Materialism, root cause of evils in Nigeria." In: Vanguard Newspaper, 16 December, 2016.

Chapter 03

[1]Albert, Isaac O. (2005). "Explaining 'godfatherism' in Nigerian Politics" in: African Sociological Review (9, (2), p.91.

[2]Ibid., p.94.

[3]Ibid., p.97.

[4]Ibid., pp.97-98.

[5]Sunday Champion (8 June, 2003). p. 11.

[6]Ngige, Chris (2003). "My problem with Uba" in: Tell, 28 July, 2003, p. 42.

[7]Albert, Isaac O. (2005). African Sociological Review (9, (2), p.91.

[8]Thenationonlineng.net "Halliburton: Four ex-Heads of State, 89 Others Indicted" >https://thenationonlineng.net/halliburton-four-ex-heads-state-89-others-indicted/

[9]Ibid.

[10]Ibid.

[11]Ibid.

[12]Ibekwe, Nicholas (3 October 2014). "Malabu Oil Deal: Corrupt Nigerian Officials Bought Private Jets, Armoured Cars With N83 Billion Bribe" Premiumtimesng.com>https://www.premiumtimesng.com/news/headlines/168992-malabu-oil-deal-corrupt-nigerian-officials-bought-private-jets-armoured-cars-with-n83-billion-bribe.html

[13]Ibid.

[14] Ibid.

[15] Ibid.

[16]Alli, Yusuf (2019). "Court Seizes N1.04b Traced To Ex-First Lady Patience Jonathan" in: The Nation, February 2, 2019, p.5.

[17]Ibid.

[18]Ibid.

[19]Okonjo-Iweala (2018). Fighting Corruption is Dangerous: The Story Behind the Headlines. Cambridge, MA: The MIT Press, p.35.

[20]Ibid., p.36.

[21]Ibid., p.37.

[22]Alli, Yusuf (2019). "Court Seizes N1.04b Traced To Ex-First Lady Patience Jonathan" in: The Nation, December9, 2019, p.10.

[23]Ibid.

[24]Okonjo-Iweala (2018). Fighting Corruption is Dangerous: The Story Behind the Headlines, p.128.

[25]Thisdaylive.com (5 February 2017). "Ibori Returns to Rousing Welcome by Kinsmen" > https://www.thisdaylive.com/index.php/2017/02/05/ibori-returns-to-rousing-welcome-by-kinsmen/

[26]Carroll, Rory (2005). "Nigerian State Governor Dresses Up To Escape £1.8m Charges in UK" theguardian.com, 23 November 2005 > https://www.theguardian.com/world/2005/nov/23/hearafrica05.development

[27]Ibid.

Chapter 04

[1]The Punch Newspaper (29 May 2016), p.2.

[2]Ibid.

[3]Ezukanma, Tochukwu (Monday 8 July 2019). "Nigeria: What Manner of Democracy?" in: The Nation, p.17.

[4]Akpan, Uwem (2016). "Corruption and its Implication on Development in Contemporary Nigeria" in: Nigeria Police Academy Journal of Humanities (Vol.1 No.1.), June 2016, p.376.

[5]Thenationonlineng.net (10 August 2019). "EFCC Begins Probe Of Obasanjo Govt's $16bn Power Project" https://thenationonlineng.net/efcc-be-gins-probe-of-obasanjo-govts-16bn-power-project/

[6]Ibid.

[7]Akpan, Uwem (2016). "Corruption and its Implication on Development in Contemporary Nigeria" in: Nigeria Police Academy Journal of Humanities (Vol.1 No.1.), p.380.

[8]Ibid., p.377.

[9]Ibid.

[10]Daily Trust (26 April 2008), p.6.

[11]Akpan, Uwem (2016). "Corruption and its Implication on Development in Contemporary Nigeria", p.378.

[12]Ibid.

[13]Okoi-Uyouyo, M. (2008). EFCC and the New Imperialism: A Study of Corruption in the Obasanjo Years. Calabar: Bookman Publishers.

[14] Akpan, Uwem (2016). "Corruption and its Implication on Development in Contemporary Nigeria", p. 378.

[15]Ibid, p.379.

[16]Ibid., pp. 378-379.
[17]Ibid., p.379.

[18]Umar, A. "How Obasanjo and Co Looted Nigeria in Eight Years." http://saharareporters.com/-colonelabubakarumar2.php

[19]Akpan, Uwem (2016), p.381.

[20]The Punch (29 May 2016).

[21]Akpan, Uwem (2016), pp.381-382.

[22] Ibid., 382.

[23] Okoi-Uyouyo, M. (2008). EFCC and the New Imperialism: A Study of Corruption in the Obasanjo Years.

[24] Ibid.

[25] The Punch (29 May 2016).

[26] Saharareporters.com (24 September 2006). "OBJ/Atiku scandal: What EFCC Failed to Disclose-TheNEWS/Saharareporters" > http://saharareporters.com/2006/09/24/objatiku-scandal-what-efcc-failed-disclose-thenewssaharareporters

[27] Ibid.

[28] Ibid.

[29] Ibid.

[30] Ibid.

[31] Ibid.

[32] Ibid.

[33] Ibid.

[34] David-West, T. (2005:63). "Building Leaders for Tomorrow: A Collective Responsibility " in: The Guardian, September 8, 2005, p.63.

[35] Ibid. pp.62-63.

[36] Orngu, C.S. (2006). Anti-Corruption Campaign in Nigeria: A Paradox. Makurdi: Aboki Publishers, p.71.

[37] The News (5 July 2004), p21.

[38] Orbunde, Emmanuel & A.O. Ogoh (2016). "Corruption, Accountability and Transparency in the Public Service: An Evaluative Analysis of the Obasanjo Administration, 1999-2007" in: International Journal of Innovative Development & Policy Studies 4 (1), January – March 2016, p.41.

[39] The News (5 July 2004), p.22.

[40] Orbunde, Emmanuel & A.O. Ogoh (2016). "Corruption, Accountability and Transparency in the Public Service: An Evaluative Analysis of the Obasanjo Administration, 1999-2007" in: International Journal of Innovative Development & Policy Studies 4 (1), January – March 2016, p.41.

[41] Thisday (1 July 2008), p.8.

[42] Akpan, Uwem (2016), p.382.

[43]Okoi-Uyouyo, M. (2008). EFCC and the New Imperialism.

[44]Ibid.

[45]Ibid.

[46]Onyemaizu, Chidiebere (2011). "Tracing Nigeria's Stolen Billions" in: The Source Magazine (Vol.29 No.19), August 29, 2011, p18.

[47]Ibid.

[48]Ibid., p.19.

[49]Ibid.

[50] Ekundayo, Kayode Ekundayo, Kayode; Lagos (31 December 2017). "Where is Tafa Balogun?". Daily Trust> https://dailytrust.com/where-is-tafa-balogun

[51] Ibid.

[52]The Punch (29 May 2016).

[53] David-West, T. (2005). "Building Leaders for Tomorrow: A Collective Responsibility " in: The Guardian, September 8, 2005, pp.25-28.

[54]Okoi-Uyouyo, M. (2008). EFCC and the New Imperialism.

[55]Akpan, Uwem (2016), pp.383-384.

[56]The cable.com(8 May 2014). "In memoriam: 5 things to remember Yar'Adua for"> https://www.thecable.ng/in-memoriam-5-things-to-remember-yaradua-for

[57]Vanguardngr.com (8 September 2011). "Yar'Adua knew Aondoakaa was corrupt but could not sack him – Wikileaks"> https://www.vanguardngr.com/2011/09/yaradua-knew-aondo-akaa-was-corrupt-but-could-not-sack-him-wikileaks/

[58]Ojo, Sunday (2016). "Looting the Looters: The Paradox of Anti-Corruption Crusades in Nigeria's Fourth Republic (1999-2014)" in: Canadian Social Science (Vol. 12, No. 9), p.7.

[59]Shirbon, Estelle (19 September 2013). "Nigerian Governor Gave $15 Million Cash Bribe In Bag, Court Hears" Reuters.com >https://www.reuters.com/article/uk-britain-nige-ria-ibori-idUKBRE98I0XD20130919

[60]Adeniyi, Olusegun (2011). Power, Politics and Death: A Front-Row Account of Nigeria Under the Late President Yar'Adua. Lagos: Kachifo Ltd., pp.19-20.

[61]Arisekola, Wole (10 December 2007). "Nigeria Attorney General Michael Aondoakaa Moves To Stall Peter Odili's Corruption Case In Port Harcourt" africanews.com > http://www.african-ews.com/site/Nigeria_Attorney_General_Aondoaka_moves_to_stall/list_messages/13775

[62]Blueprint.ng (15 August 2019). "Nigerians Petition EFCC, Demand Arrest, Prosecution of Ex-AGF, Aondoakaa in 7 Days"> https://www.blueprint.ng/nigerians-petition-efcc-demand-ar-

rest-prosecution-of-ex-agf-aondoakaa-in-7-days/

[63]Adeniyi, Olusegun (2011), p.16.

[64]Alli, Yusuf (19 March 2020). "Ex-Rivers Governor Odili under probe for N100b 'Fraud'" thenationonlineng.net> https://thenationonlineng.net/ex-rivers-governor-odili-un-der-probe-for-n100b-fraud/

[65]Ibid.

[66]Arisekola, Wole (10 December 2007). "Nigeria Attorney General Michael Aondoakaa Moves To Stall Peter Odili's Corruption Case In Port Harcourt" africanews.com > http://www.african-ews.com/site/Nigeria_Attorney_General_Aondoaka_moves_to_stall/list_messages/13775

[67]Ibid.

[68]Mojeed, Musikilu (27 February 2012). "How Ibori, The Thief In Government House, Admitted Stealing $250million" premiumtimesng.com > https://www.premium-timesng.com/news/3972-how-ibori-the-thief-in-government-house-admitted-stealing-250million.html

[69]Ibid.

[70]Ibid.

[71]Ojo, Sunday (2016). "Looting the Looters: The Paradox of Anti-Corruption Crusades in Nigeria's Fourth Republic (1999-2014), p.9.

[72]Saharareporters.com (30 December 2008). "Igbinedion Gets Easy Plea-Bargain: No Jail Time, Keeps Billions In Stolen Funds, Keeps Vast Properties"> http://saharareport-ers.com/2008/12/30/igbinedi-on-gets-easy-plea-bargain-no-jail-time-keeps-billions-stolen-funds-keeps-vast

[73]Ibid.

[74]Ibid.

[75]Eboh, Camillus (5 August 2008). "Nigeria Charges 9th Ex-Governor With Embezzlement" > https://www.reuters.com/article/nigeria-corruption-governor-idUSL571733320080805

[76] Ibid.

[77]Icirnigeria.org (25 July 2020). "Diepreye Alamieyeseigha" > https://www.icirnigeria.org/diepr-eye-alamieyeseigha/

[78]Thecable.ng (11 October 2015). "Alamieyeseigha Built Just One House… He Was Never A Corrupt Man, Says Ibori" > https://www.thecable.ng/alamieyeseigha-just-one-house-nev-er-corrupt-says-ibori

[79]Voanews.com (1 November 2009). "Nigerian House Speaker Resigns Over Corruption Scandal" > https://www.voanews.com/archive/nigerian-house-speaker-resigns-over-corruption-scandal

[80]Saharareporters.com (30 October 2007). "Etteh, Deputy Resign After Humiliation" > http://saharareporters.com/2007/10/30/etteh-deputy-resign-after-humiliation

[81]Ekundayo, Kayode; Lagos (31 December 2017). "Where is Tafa Balogun?". Daily Trust> https://dailytrust.com/where-is-tafa-balogun

[82]Ibid.

[83]Ibid.

[84]Orilade, Tony (9 October 2008). "Ex-NAMA Boss Charged With Fraud" Onlinenigeria.com > https://onlinenigeria.com/nm/templates/?a=13738

[85]Ibid.

[86]Reuters.com (25 March 2008). "Two Nigerian Ministers Resign Over Graft Charges"> https://www.reuters.com/article/nigeria-corruption-ministers-idUKL2551982920080325

[87]Ibid.

[88]Saharareporters.com (12 December 2017). "Nigeria Lost $32bn To Corruption Under Former President Jonathan – DFID" > http://saharareporters.com/2017/12/12/nigeria-lost-32bn-corruption-under-former-president-jonathan-%E2%80%93-dfid

[89]Okonjo-Iweala (2018). Fighting Corruption is Dangerous: The Story Behind the Headlines. Cambridge, MA: The MIT Press, p.34.

[90]Ibid., p.35.

[91]Ibid.

[92]Ibid., p.36.

[93]Ibid., p.35.

[94]Ibid., p.36.

[95]Ibid., pp.36-37.

[96]Ibid., p.44.

[97]Ibid., p.46.
[98]Ibid., p.47.

[99]Ibid., p.48.

[100]Ameh, John et al (2015). "'Missing' $20billion: Reps Issue Fresh Ultimatum to Okonjo-Iweala" The Nation, Thursday 26 February, 2015, p.2.

[101] Sotubo, Monjola (12 April 2017). "12 Things You Should Know About The Controversial Malabu Oil Deal" Pulse.ng > https://www.pulse.ng/news/local/malabu-oil-scam-12-things-you-should-know-about-controversial-deal/p0lq57g

[102]Ibid.

[103]Ibid.

[104]Okonjo-Iweala (2018). Fighting Corruption is Dangerous, p.33.

[105]Ibid.

[106]Akpan, Uwem (2016). "Corruption and its Implication on Development in Contemporary Nigeria", p.386.

[107]Sotubo, Monjola (7 December 2015). Ex-Minister Diezani Might Have Personally Supervised The Looting Of $6 Billion" > https://www.pulse.ng/news/local/diezani-ex-minister-might-have-personally-supervised-stealing-of-dollar6bn-video/edxh0m1

[108]Olufemi , Alfred (10 August 2020). "Diezani, wanted for massive corruption, laments decay in societal values in Nigeria" premiumtimesng.com > https://www.premiumtimesng.com/news/top-news/407846-diezani-wanted-for-massive-corruption-laments-decay-in-societal-values-in-nigeria.html

[109]Kazeem, Yomi (8 August 2017). "Nigeria Has Seized A $37.5 Million Luxury Apartment Complex From Its Ex-Oil Minister" qz.com > https://qz.com/africa/1049026/diezani-alison-madueke-corruption-nigeria-has-seized-a-37-5-million-luxury-apartment-complex-from-its-ex-oil-minister/

[110]Ibid.

[111]Ibid.

[112]World Peace Foundation "Nigeria's Armsgate Scandal". https://sites.tufts.edu/corruptarmsdeals/nigerias-armsgate-scandal/

[113]pmnewsnigeria.com (11 January 2016). "Dasukigate: 'Who Got What' From $2.1bn Arms Deal">https://pmnewsnigeria.com/2016/01/11/dasukigate-who-got-what-from-2-1bn-arms-deal/

[114]BBC (1 December 2015). "Nigeria's Dasuki 'Arrested Over $2bn Arms Fraud'" > https://www.bbc.com/news/world-africa-34973872

[115]Sanni, Kunle (26 November 2020). "How Maina stole N14 billion using fictitious accounts — EFCC" > https://www.premiumtimesng.com/news/top-news/428192-how-maina-stole-n14-billion-using-fictitious-accounts-efcc.html

[116]Ibid.

[117] Vanguardngr.com (11 December 2019). "Alleged pension scam: How Maina Illegally Acquired Property In Son's Name — EFCC Witness" > https://www.vanguardngr.com/2019/12/alleged-pension-scam-how-maina-illegally-acquired-property-in-sons-name-efcc-witness

[118]Ibid.

[119]Abolade, Lukman (3 December 2020). "Pension Fraud: Police Extradites Wanted MAINA From Niger Republic" icirnigeria.org > https://www.icirnigeria.org/pension-fraud-police-extradites-wanted-maina-from-niger-republic/

[120]Okonjo-Iweala (2018). Fighting Corruption is Dangerous, p.96.

[121]Ibid.

[122]Premiumtimesng.com (28 January 2013). "Director jailed 2yrs for stealing N33bn pension fund freed on N250,000 Fine" > https://www.premiumtimesng.com/news/117599-director-jailed-2yrs-for-stealing-n33bn-pension-fund-freed-on-n250000-fine.html

[123]Ibid.

[124]Odoh, Innocent (23 June 2020). "EFCC re-arrests John Yusuf for N32.8bn Pension Fraud" businessday.ng> https://businessday.ng/news/article/efcc-re-arrests-john-yusuf-for-n32-8bn-pension-fraud/

[125]Okonjo-Iweala (2018). Fighting Corruption is Dangerous, p.97.
[126]Odoh, Innocent (23 June 2020). "EFCC re-arrests John Yusuf for N32.8bn Pension Fraud" businessday.ng> https://businessday.ng/news/article/efcc-re-arrests-john-yusuf-for-n32-8bn-pension-fraud/

[127] Adesomoju, Ade (16 February 2021). "REVEALED: How Stella Oduah, CCECC, Others Laundered N5 Billion – EFCC" premiumtimesng.com > https://www.premiumtimesng.com/news/-headlines/443108-re-vealed-how-nigerian-senator-stella-oduah-chinese-firm-ccecc-others-laundered-n5billion-in-five-months-efcc.html

[128]Ibid.

[129]Ogundipe, Samuel (21 June 2017). "N255 Million Bulletproof Car Scandal: Efcc To Grill Stella Oduah" Premiumtimesng.com > https://www.premium-timesng.com/news/more-news/234702-n255-mil-lion-bulletproof-car-scandal-efcc-grill-stella-oduah.html

[130]Channels Television (4 December 2020). "NIS Recruitment Scam: Nepotism, Lopsidedness Derailed Exercise – Moro Tells Court". Channelstv.com > https://www.channel-stv.com/2020/12/04/nis-recruitment-scam-ne-potism-lopsidedness-derailed-exercise-moro-tells-court/

[131]Ibid.

[132]Ibid.

[133]Vanguardngr.com (30 September 2014). "$9.3m Arms Deal: Oritsejafor Opens Up"> https://www.vanguardngr.com/2014/09/9-3m-arms-deal-oritsejafor-opens/

[134]The Nation (7 October 2014). "Bad Arms Deal: Nigeria Loses $5.7m More to South Africa" p.1.

[135]Ibid.

[136] Ibekwe, Nicholas (15 October 2014). "We can't return Nigeria's seized $15Million arms money without due process – South Africa" > https://www.premiumtimesng.com/news/headlines/169486-we-cant-return-nigerias-seized-15million-arms-money-without-due-process-south-africa.html

[137]Ojo, Sunday (2016). "Looting the Looters: The Paradox of Anti-Corruption Crusades in Nigeria's
Fourth Republic (1999-2014)" in: Canadian Social Science
(Vol. 12, No. 9), p.9.
[138]Godwin, Ameh (10 February 2018). "Strange Snake Swallows N36 Million Cash In Jamb Office" dailypost.ng > https://dailypost.ng/2018/02/10/strange-snake-swallows-n36-million-cash-jamb-office/

[139]Ibid.

[140]vanguardngr.com (21 February 2018). "Shocker! Monkeys swallow N70m Belonging to Northern Senators" > https://www.vanguardngr.com/2018/02/just-monkeys-swallow-n70m-belonging-northern-senators/

[141]Rahman, Abdur (17 June 2019). "Nigeria probing how gorilla swallowed over $19,000 Zoo Funds" africanews.com > https://www.africanews.com/2019/06/17/nigeria-probing-how-gorilla-swallowed-over-19000-zoo-funds/

[142]Omeje, Chikezie (30 October 2017). "UPDATED: Buhari sacks Babachir Lawal, Ayo Oke" Icirnigeria.org>https://www.icirnigeria.org/buhari-sacks-babchir-lawal-ayo-oke-appoints-new-sgf/

[143]Tsa, Godwin (30 November 2020). "N544 million Grass-Cutting Contract: Ex-SGF Babachir Lawal, Others Re-Arraigned" Sunnewsonline.com> https://www.sunnewsonline.com/n544-million-grass-cutting-contract-ex-sgf-babachir-lawal-others-re-arraigned/

[144]Ibrahim, Idris (1 November 2017). "$43 Million Ikoyi Money: EFCC Summons Ex-NIA Chief Oke, Wife" Premiumtimesng.com > https://www.premiumtimesng.com/news/headlines/248041-43-million-ikoyi-money-efcc-summons-ex-nia-chief-oke-wife.html

[145] Ibid.

[146]Fashola, Lere(30 May 2018). "Court orders Buhari to probe N481b Budget Padding Claim" esq-law.com> https://esq-law.com/court-orders-buhari-to-probe-n481b-budget-padding-claim.html

[147]Ibid.

[148]Kabir, Adejumo (16 August 2020). "Nigerians Criticise Ganduje Over Comment On Corruption" premiumtimesng.com > https://www.premiumtimesng.com/news/top-news/409089-nigerians-criticise-ganduje-over-comment-on-corruption.html

[149]Ibid.

[150]Ibid.

[151]Garba, Ramatu (7 July 2021). "Ganduje Withdraws 'Gandollar' Defamation Suit, To Pay

N800k Costs" Pmnewsnigeria.com > https://pmnewsnigeria.com/2021/07/07/ganduje-with-draws-gandollar-defamation-suit-to-pay-n800k-costs/

[152]Arogbofa, Ebi (11 September 2020). "NDDC: President Buhari Should Act on the IMC Indictment for Corruption" Guardian.ng > https://guardian.ng/features/focus/nddc-president-buhari-should-act-on-the-imc-indictment-for-corruption/

[153]Ibid.

[154]Ibid.

[155]Egbas, Jude (23 July 2020). "Honourable Minister It Is Not Okay" Pulse.ng>https://www.-pulse.ng/news/local/honourable-minister-it-is-not-okay-pulse-editors-opinion/zsvm0pf

[156]Omonobi, Kingsley (21 October 2016). "N500m MTN Bribery Allegation: Presidency Orders Probe of Abba Kyari" Vanguardngr.com > https://www.vanguardn-gr.com/2016/10/n500m-mtn-bribery-allegation-presidency-orders-probe-of-abba-kyari/

[157]Opejobi, Seun (20 September 2016). "Buhari Reportedly Receives Evidence Showing Chief of Staff, Kyari Took N500m bribe from MTN" dailypost.ng> https://dailypost.ng/2016/09/20/bihari-reportedly-receives-evidence-showing-chief-staff-kyari-took-n500m-bribe-mtn/

[158]Omonobi, Kingsley (21 October 2016). "N500m MTN Bribery Allegation: Presidency Orders Probe of Abba Kyari" Vanguardngr.com > https://www.vanguardn-gr.com/2016/10/n500m-mtn-bribery-allegation-presidency-orders-probe-of-abba-kyari/

[159]Ibid.

[160]Opejobi, Seun (20 September 2016). "Buhari Reportedly Receives Evidence Showing Chief of Staff, Kyari Took N500m bribe from MTN" dailypost.ng> https://dailypost.ng/2016/09/20/bihari-reportedly-receives-evidence-showing-chief-staff-kyari-took-n500m-bribe-mtn/

[161] Anti-Corruption and Research Based Data Initiative (January 7, 2019). Petition on suspected Financial Crimes And Breaches Of The Code Of Conduct Bureau Requirements Against Honourable Mr. Justice W. S. Nkanu Onnoghen addressed to Code of Conduct Bureau, Abuja.

[162]Ogundipe, Samuel (12 January 2019). "EXCLUSIVE: The full corruption charges against Chief Justice Walter Onnoghen" Premiumtimesng.com > https://www.premium-timesng.com/news/headlines/305388-exclu-sive-the-full-corruption-charges-against-chief-justice-walter-onnoghen.html

[163]Alhassan, Rayyan (12 January 2019). "DOCUMENTS: How Onnoghen Admits 'Forgetting' To Declare Assets" Dailynigerian.com > https://dailynigerian.com/documents-how-onnoghen-ad-mits-forgetting-to-declare-assets/

[164]Ibid.

[165]Omohomhion, Felix (18 Apr 2019). "CCT Finds Onnoghen Guilty Of False Asset Declaration". Businessday.ng > https://businessday.ng/news/article/cct-sacks-onnogh-en-as-chief-justice-of-nigeria/

[166]Olawoyin, Oladeinde (21 April 2021). "Nigeria's Management Of COVID-19 Fund Lacks

'Framework for Accountability' – Budgit" Premiumtimesng.com > https://www.premium-timesng.com/news/more-news/456659-nige-rias-management-of-covid-19-fund-lacks-framework-for-accountability-budgit.html

[167]Ibid.

[168] Fasan, Olu (16 April 2020). "COVID-19 is a fertile ground for aggravated corruption in Nigeria". Vanguardngr.com> https://www.vanguardngr.com/2020/04/covid-19-is-a-fer-tile-ground-for-aggravated-corruption-in-nigeria/

[169]Premiumtimesng.com (11 July 2020). "Magu: Report Says Interest on N550 bn Re-looted" > https://www.premiumtimesng.com/news/headlines/402475-magu-re-port-says-interest-on-n550-bn-re-looted.html

[170]Ibid.

[171]Africanews.com (14 May 2021). "Nigeria President's Son-in-Law Wanted in Fraud Probe" > https://www.africanews.com/2021/05/14/nigeria-president-s-son-in-law-wanted-in-fraud-probe//

[172]Ibid.

[173]Saharareporters.com (7 May 2021). "EXPOSED: How NPA Director, Hadiza Usman, Was Removed Over Dubious Lebanese Contract Involving Lawan, Amaechi, Malami" > http://saha-rareporters.com/2021/05/07/exposed-how-npa-direc-tor-hadiza-usman-was-removed-over-dubious-lebanese-contract

[174]Ibid.

[175]Ibid.

[176]Saharareporters.com (26 May 2021). "EXCLUSIVE: Audit Report Exposes N18 Billion Fraudulent Expenditure Under Suspended NPA MD, Hadiza Usman In 2017" > http://saha-rareporters.com/2021/05/26/exclusive-audit-re-port-exposes-n18-billion-fraudulent-expenditure-under-suspended-npa-md

Chapter 05

[1]Duru, Innocent (14 December 2019). "Row Over Execution Of Multi-Million Naira Constituency Projects" in: The Nation Newspaper, p.18.

[2]Ibid.

[3]Ochigbo, Franca & Bennett Atumah (9 December 2019). "Nigeria Losing Billions To Intervention Projects" in: The Nations Newspaper, p.20.

[4]Iredia, Tonnie (24 April 2016). "What Exactly Is The Meaning of Constituency Project?" Vanguardngr.com>https://.www.vanguardngr.com/2016/04/exactly-meaning-constituency-project/

[5]Ochigbo, Franca & Bennett Atumah (9 December 2019). "Nigeria Losing Billions To Intervention Projects" in: The Nations Newspaper, p.20.

[6]Olafusi, Ebunoluwa (15 December 2019). "ICPC: How Lawmakers Embezzle Funds Meant for Constituency Projects". Thecable.ng > https://www.thecable.ng/icpc-how-lawmakers-embezzle-funds-meant-for-constituency-projects

[7]Ibid.

[8]Ibid.

[9]Ibid.

[10]Ibid.

[11] Akinpelu, Yusuf (18 January 2020). "EXCLUSIVE: Top 20 Agencies Nigerian Lawmakers Will Use To Siphon 'Free Money' In 2020" premiumtimesng.com > https://www.premium-timesng.com/news/headlines/373145-exclu-sive-top-20-agencies-nigerian-lawmakers-will-use-to-siphon-free-money-in-2020.html

[12]Ibid.

[13]Ibid.

[14] BudgIT (N.D.). Proposed 2019 Budget: Frivolous & Suspicious Items Prepared for National Assembly.

[15]@TrackaNG posted in February 2021 on Twitter.
[16]@TrackaNG posted on 17 February 2021 on Twitter.

[17]Sunday, Eno-Abasi (5 April 2020). "Constituency Projects: Still A Long Way To Getting Value For Money" Guardian.ng > https://guardian.ng/saturday-magazine/cover/constituency-pro-jects-still-a-long-way-to-getting-value-for-money/

[18]Ibid.

[19]Ibid.

[20]Ibid.

[21]Ibid.

Chapter 06

[1]Premiumtimesng.com (4 February 2017). "Celebration In Delta As Ibori Arrives Hometown" > https://www.premiumtimesng.com/news/top-news/222558-celebra-tion-delta-ibori-arrives-hometown.html

[2]Ibid.

[3]Ibid.

[4]Human Rights Watch (25 August 2011). "Corruption on Trial?: The Record of Nigeria's Economic and Financial Crimes Commission" Hrw.org > https://www.hrw.org/re-port/2011/08/25/corruption-trial/record-nigerias-economic-and-financial-crimes-commission

[5]Saharareporters.com (30 December 2008). "Igbinedion Gets Easy Plea-Bargain: No Jail Time, Keeps Billions In Stolen Funds, Keeps Vast Properties" > http://saharareport-ers.com/2008/12/30/igbinedi-on-gets-easy-plea-bargain-no-jail-time-keeps-billions-stolen-funds-keeps-vast

[6]Saharareporters.com (30 April 2008). "Court Fines Igbinedion N3m For N25bn Scam" > http://saharareporters.com/2015/04/30/court-fines-igbinedion-n3m-n25bn-scam

[7] Ekundayo, Kayode (31 December 2017). "Where is Tafa Balogun?". Daily Trust > https://daily-trust.com/where-is-tafa-balogun

[8]Ibid.

[9]Kabir, Adejumo (6 July 2019). "How EFCC, AGF's strange 'Romance' Saved Goje After Surrendering Senate Presidency Bid". Premiumtimesng.com > https://www.premium-timesng.com/news/headlines/339222-how-ef-cc-agfs-strange-romance-saved-goje-after-surrendering-senate-presidency-bid.html

[10]Abolade, Lukman (20 February 2021). "Tafa Balogun, Olisa Metuh and Other Prominent Nigerians Who Own Properties in Dubai". Icirnigeria.org > https://www.icirnigeria.org/tafa-balo-gun-olisa-metuh-and-other-prominent-nigerians-who-own-properties-in-dubai/

[11]Sanni, Kunle (29 December 2020). "High Profile Corruption Cases Nigerians expect in 2021"Premiumtimesng.com> https://www.premiumtimesng.com/news/top-news/433732-high-pro-file-corruption-cases-nigerians-expect-in-2021.html

[12]Abolade, Lukman (20 February 2021). > https://www.icirnigeria.org/tafa-balogun-oli-sa-metuh-and-other-prominent-nigerians-who-own-properties-in-dubai/

[13]The Nation (26 June 2014). "Interminable Probes: The EFCC and the Courts Should Not Turn the Graft Cases into a Cynical Theatre", p.17.

[14]Owasanoye, Bolaji (2014). Justice Or Impunity: High Profile Corruption Cases Crawling Or Gone To Sleep. Lagos: Human Development Initiative, p.5.

[15]Ibid.

[16]Tran, M. (17 April 2012). "Former Nigerian State Governor James Ibori Receives 13-year

Sentence" Guardian (UK) > http://www.guardian.co.uk/global-development/2012/apr/17/nigeria-governor-james-ibori-sentenced

[17]Human Rights Watch (25 August 2011). "Corruption on Trial?: The Record of Nigeria's Economic and Financial Crimes Commission". Hrw.org > https://www.hrw.org/report/2011/08/25/corruption-trial/record-nigerias-economic-and-financial-crimes-commission

[18]Alli, Yusuf (2016). "Alleged N36b Fraud: EFCC Storms Ex-Governor Turaki's Abuja Home" in: The Nation Newspaper, May 19, 2016, p.10.

[19]Ibid.

[20]Owasanoye, Bolaji (2014). Justice Or Impunity: High Profile Corruption Cases Crawling Or Gone To Sleep, pp.9-10.

[21]Ezeamalu, Ben (5 March 2014). "After 7 Years, Corruption Trial of Former Enugu Governor, Nnamani, Yet To Begin", PremiumTimes > www.premiumtimesng.com/news/156201-7-years-corruption-trial-former-enugu-governor-nnamani-yet-begin.html

[22]Adesomoju, Ade (5 March 2014). "Nnamani's Lawyer Stalls N4.5b Money Laundering Trial", Punch> www.punchng.com/news/nnamanis-lawyer-stalls-n4-5bn-money-laundering-trial/)

[23]Braithwaite, Onikepo & Jude Igbanoi (2021). "With 10,000 Pending Appeals, the Supreme Court is Overworked" in: ThisDay Newspaper, Tuesday 17 August 2021, pp.viii-x.

Chapter 07

[1]Adeniyi, Olusegun (2011). Power, Politics and Death: A Front-Row Account of Nigeria Under the Late President Yar'Adua. Lagos: Kachifo Ltd., p.21.

[2]Human Rights Watch (25 August 2011). "Corruption on Trial? The Record of Nigeria's Economic and Financial Crimes Commission" > https://www.hrw.org/report/2011/08/25/corruption-trial/record-nigerias-economic-and-financial-crimes-commission

[3]Nwogu, Success et al (18 January 2019). "ICYMI: Oshiomhole: Once You Join The APC, Your Sins Are Forgiven" punchng.com > https://punchng.com/oshiomhole-once-you-join-the-apc-your-sins-are-forgiven/

[4]Okonjo-Iweala (2018). Fighting Corruption is Dangerous: The Story Behind the Headlines, p.128.

[5]Alliyu, Nurudeen (July 2014). "Nigeria's Cobweb of Corruption and the Path to Underdevelopment" in: An International Journal Of Arts And Humanities (Ijah) (Vol.3)(3), p.110 Available at http://dx.doi.org/10.4314/ijah.v3i3.9

[6]Onyekwere, Joseph (26 January 2021). "ICPC Corruption Verdict Unsettles Judiciary" Guardian.ng> https://guardian.ng/features/law/icpc-corruption-verdict-unsettles-judiciary/

[7]Ibid.

[8]Vanguardngr.com (26 November 26, 2019). "Nigerian politicians Don't Believe in God –Tsav" > https://www.vanguardngr.com/2019/11/nigerian-politicians-dont-believe-in-god-tsav/

[9]Bassey, Ben (18 April 2018). "EFCC, ICPC Secure Only 10 High Profile Convictions in 17 Years, Says Don" pulse.ng > https://www.pulse.ng/news/local/efcc-icpc-secure-only-10-high-profile-convictions-in-17-years-says-don/yqsyn82

[10]Jibueze, Joseph (3 September 2013). "Politicians Should Not Appoint Judges, Says Appeal Court Justice"
In: Thenationonlineng.net > https://thenationonlineng.net/politicians-should-not-appoint-judges-says-appeal-court-justice/

[11]Unodc.org. "The main factors aimed at securing judicial independence"> https://www.unodc.org/e4j/en/crime-prevention-criminal-justice/module-14/key-issues/1--the-main-factors-aimed-at-securing-judicial-independence.html